THE FENG SHUI JOURNEY OF MR ALEISTER CROWLEY

MARLENE PACKWOOD

CONTENTS

PAGE

THE FENG SHUI OF MR ALEISTER CROWLEY

From the 'Tao Te Ching' by Aleister Crowley

"The Nature of the Tao"
"The Tao-Path is not the All-Tao
The Name is not the Thing Named
Unmanifested, it is the Secret Father of Heaven and Earth,
Manifested it is their Mother.
To Understand this Mystery, one must be fulfilling one's will,
And if one is not thus free,
One will gain but a smattering of it.
The Tao is one, and the Teh but a phase thereof.
The abyss of this Mystery is the Portal of Serpent-Wonder.

The Tao

The Teh — The Tao
Source of the Mother — Source of the Father

Heaven - Ch'ien

Fire — Water-Tui

Sun

Air-Sun — Earth-Ken

Moon - K'an
Earth - k'un"

The Way of the Tao is threaded throughout the philosophy of Feng Shui. It was written by a Librarian Lao Tsu between the 4th to 7th centuries as is known. It means the Book of The Way and its Power. It offers the Way of the Watercourse. Thus Taoism is the Way of Man's co-operation with Nature. Its Way is learn by observing Nature. Lao Tsu wrote, "The Tao is like an empty pitcher. Poured from, but never drained. Infinitely deep, it is the Source of all things.
It blunts the sharp,   It unties the knotted
Shade's the bright
Unites with all Dust
Dimly seen, yet eternally present,
I do not know who gave birth to it
It is older than any conception of God".
Aleister Crowley's interpretation of the Tao Te Ching is of a world in constant motion. In some ways he stands by the original and in others, seeks to interpret Lao Tsu's wisdom. The World is not tidy and neat and everything doesn't always work out as planned. All we can do is observe and learn from Cosmic Laws such as that of Yin and Yang, The Law of opposites, and the Way of the Watercourse. Lao Tsu says,
"The virtue of a house is to be well placed; of the mind, to be at ease in Silence as in Space; of societies, to be well disposed; of governments, to maintain quietude...............Gold and jade endanger the house of their possessor. Wealth and honours lead to arrogance and envy, and bring ruin.."

Mr Aleister Crowley was born Edward Alexander Crowley at 30 Clarendon Square, Leamington Spa, in Warwickshire on October 12 1875. A Libran with Leo rising and the Moon in Pisces. He was born into an affluent home in a Square in the North of the Town, though the house was favourably South facing.

Here a red car is directly outside the front door to No 30 in 2010. From Such a favourable address, in a square and on a hill facing South we Would expect the occupants to be ambitious and fortunate in Life. The front door in the South promotes growth and creativity and is the area of Fame in the Lo Shu (or magic Square) and holds the No9. There are nine houses in the Lo Shu and these make up the Pa Kua. Feng Shui seeks a balance in all 9.
As you can see on a basic level, the Way of the Tao is the spiritual practice and Feng Shui is its practical application and discipline in the home and work

Clarendon Square, Leamington Spa

environment, garden or other area of life. Feng Shui creates clear energy through positive Chi; the 'dragons breath' - propitious energy throughout the home.

Aleister at first attended the Ebor School; a Plymouth Brethren School in Cambridge. Here, after his father's death he rejected Christianity and the hypocrisy and cruelty of its masters and ethos. He was accused at the Ebor School of a crime he knew nothing about and thus forced to live on bread and water. Eventually he broke down and the strain and misery had affected his kidneys. After this a series of tutors taught Crowley for a while. He had interesting adventures with them and went fishing and triumphantly learned to masturbate. Aleister went on to attend Malvern School in 1891 where his Mother sent him to get fresh air and play sports. He remained there for 3 terms but failed to win academic prizes. Thus he invented hardships which he related to his Mother so that she took him out of the school.

Malvern School

In 1892, Aleister attended Tonbridge School for the Spring, Summer and Autumn terms. Crowley was now 16 and feeling on better form. He had intelligence but lack the application of hard work here. Now he had discovered sex and caught gonorrhea from a Glasgow Prostitute. He was embarrassed by this and was most likely expelled from Tonbridge for it though he never admitted it in his 'Confessions'.

Tonbridge School

This time Aleister was moved by his Mother to Eastbourne College (below) where he was happier. He lived with a tutor from the Brethren and attended day classes. He liked Chemistry, French and Literature. It was at Eastbourne that Crowley came to like rock climbing and also joined the chess team. Crowley scaled the 4 highest fells in Langdale and one of his favourite places to climb was Beachy Head. Here was a young man full of the promise of youth. "Camp Life...is the best life I know. The mere feeling of being in the fresh air under the stars when one goes to sleep and waking with the dawn........"

Eastbourne School 1893 - 1895

THE HEADY DAYS OF CAMBRIDGE UNIVERSITY

In 1895, Aleister Crowley attended Trinity College, Cambridge for 3 years, reading English Literature and later Mathematics and the Classics. He lived at 16 St John Street, Cambridge and these years were to be amongst the happiest of his life. Cambridge is in the East and has always been a fountain of knowledge and an environment of openness and freedom. The East in the Pa Kua is the area of Children and creativity. At Cambridge, Crowley flourished.

Trinity College, Cambridge

If one were to place the Pa Kua over a map of Cambridge we would find that the centre would correspond to the Number 5 the Health Sector. This is the very heart of Cambridge and an area where Crowley studied and worked. His life was active, social, busy, studious and creative. Cambridge has always been a progressive town with creative and intellectual people at its core. Aleister Crowley fitted into this environment completely and met new friends and like minded people. He became flamboyant in style and dress wearing silk shirts and floppy bow ties not to mention rings set with semi precious stones.
He became a member of a debating society, The Magpie & Stump and also of the Chess Club. He also started to travel and went to St Petersburg whilst learning Russian during 1897. Crowley fell in love at this time with Jerome Pollit a former student, dancer and female impersonator who worked at the Footlights Dramatic Club. They became lovers. Certainly these 3 years were the happiest and healthiest of Crowley's entire Life. It was at 14 Trinity Street that Pollitt and Crowley lived together for a time. He had moved there from 16 St John Street which was close by. In the main room he built a magical space for ritual within a circle of white marble stones. Through Pollitt Crowley met Aubrey Beardsley in 1898. He began to write poetry and take it seriously. He was self published through Leonard Smithers who also published Oscar Wilde. His relationship with Pollitt suffered due to Pollitt's lack of outlook on the Spiritual side of Life and lack of interest in Magic. It is to be noted that the notorious poems 'White Stains' were published during 1898. Unfortunately Smithers went bankrupt in 1899.

Cambridge as a University town, stands on the edge of the Fens and in the East of England. Being in the East it relates to the Pa Kua or Bagua as the area for Wood, Family & health. Crowley began to create his own family here and to feel a sense of belonging. For him it was a place of decision and development.

Here we see the Tudor frontage of 14 Trinity Street, Cambridge where Crowley took rooms in January 1898 and lived with Herbert Charles Pollitt known to friends as Jerome. Pollitt was four years older than Crowley and an actor and entertainer as well as dancer and female impersonator at the Footlights Dramatic Club. Crowley was entranced, but shameful of his homosexual feelings, though it was Pollitt who encouraged his Poetry. They parted when Crowley left Cambridge.

Initially Crowley had taken rooms at 16 St John's Street overlooking St John's Chapel. The shop occupying that position and rooms above are shown below.

Youthful Crowley

Sydney Street, Cambridge

He also spent some time at 35 Sidney Street a street close by, in his final year. But most of the time was at 14 Trinity Street. Many of the buildings locally are owned by the University and certainly he would have been advised where to stay as a student. So his student days came to an end in May 1898 as did this carefree time in Crowley's life, and, although he did not then know it, this was the final chapter in his financial security. Calling himself Aleister Crowley instead of Alick, he strode out into the World and to London to court Fame and Fortune.

Aleister had, before leaving Cambridge formed a friendship with Gerald Kelly, a painter, in 1898. However another very important friendship was also formed that Summer with Oscar Eckenstein, 16 years older than Crowley and a mountain climber. Eckenstein was a socialist and eccentric and worked as a railway engineer. His passion was for mountaineering and in 1892 he was a member of an expedition lead by Sir William Conway to the Karakoan range in the Himalayas. Crowley may have met him at the Alpine Club and shared with him an admiration for the writings of Sir Richard Burton. That Summer they went climbing together in the Alps to Geant Zermatt.

Geant Zermatt

From this high and clear terrain he met another person who was to prove influential in introducing him to those who followed the esoteric paths. That man was Julian Baker, an analytical chemist and practical alchemist. Then back in London, Julian introduced Crowley to George Cecil Jones another chemist & follower of Magic. From Jones, Crowley first learnt of practical Magic. It was also through Jones that Crowley learnt of 'The Book of the Sacred Magic of Abra-Melin the Mage'. On 18 November 1898 Crowley was initiated into the Hermetic Order of the Golden Dawn at Mark Masons Hall, London. His magical name became Perdurabo, and he decided to perform the ritual of the Abra-melin.

Crowley moved from the Hotel Cecil, where he was staying temporarily to Chancery Lane in December 1898. Here he undertook Studies in Magic & Ritual. Crowley also met Allan Bennett at the Golden Dawn. Allan was a brilliant magician and also a chemist also suffering from asthma like Crowley. He took opium to alleviate the asthma, then morphine and also cocaine and so developed high tolerance levels to these drugs. Crowley was beguiled by Bennett and invited him to live with him in Chancery Lane. Though they were never lovers because Bennett was a Buddhist and aesthete who had rejected sex, they became close friends and magical partners. Both experimented with drugs for the purposed of altered consciousness.

LONDON 1898

Chancery Lane 2010

Crowley's flat faced South East an auspicious direction of Feng Shui for Wealth & prosperity. It is a Green area in the Pa Kua relating to Wood and growth. Crowley was comfortably off at this time and embarked on the magical working of the Abra-Melin with the assistance of Allan Bennett. Through the Golden Dawn he met William Butler Yeats an accomplished and recognised poet. One of Crowley's ambitions was to succeed as a poet. Crowley gave Yeats some poems he had written 'Jephthah' and 'Mysteries Lyrical and Dramatic' to read. Yeats was critical of these poems when all Crowley had sought was constructive advice on poetry. An element of animosity arose between them and Crowley understood that W B Yeats really did not really like him or his poems. From then on the differences between them lead to personal attacks within the Order of the Golden Dawn.

However a new Century beckoned. Crowley wished to become more accomplished in Magic and also to perform the magic of the Abra-Melin Ritual. To this end he bought a property in Scotland on Loch Ness - Boleskine House, in August 1899 and moved there in November 1899. Here Magic and Feng Shui coincide. The front door of this house faced North the area of Kan, and Water, governing Career according to the eight Life Aspirations of the Pa Kua. North was also necessary for the accomplishment of the Abra-Melin. The Loch nestling beneath Boleskine House brought beneficial chi to the dwelling. The forests behind it protected it from severe winds and harsh weather. It was far enough from the shore to prevent flooding, and high enough to give a beneficial view of the loch and surrounding mountains. This home was to provide Crowley with a new security for both family and career goals and was to be one of the places he lived in for the longest time in his life.

FRONT DOOR BOLESKINE HOUSE

BOLESKINE HOUSE

Mists coming off the Loch would have been resplendent with beneficial chi. The New and full moons would have seemed mystical, reflected in the waters. There is a harmony here of Yin and Yang which calls out for this to become a Family home. We would have to say that this was an East house as the main dwelling faces East and the rising Sun, the area, for family, relationships and health. In ancient times in China properly sited houses were backed by mountains and faced rivers or water. The true front of the house is where the natural chi can concentrate and gather, here both East and North. The Sleeping Dragon, Feng Shui would recognise as being above the house and the rounded hills are Earth and the forest Wood indicating a solid environment of balanced elements cocooning the property.
This house has excellent Feng Shui. Crowley moved into it in a busy and distracted time of his life when he was focused on achieving magical power and status. Controversy in the Order of the Golden Dawn distracted him from completing the Abra-Melin which was an on-off operation at best. His attention span waned and he could not finish what he had made an oath to do.

He went back to London and there met Elaine Simpson a poet at 36 Blythe Road, the address of the Second Order of the Adepts of the Golden Dawn. He was refused permission to enter. Furiously he went off to Paris , there to find MacGregor Mathers, Head of the Order, and inform him of what had taken place.

A local café beneath the flats at 36 Blythe Road, London SW. today.

ALWAYS PARIS

As if a cannon had launched him into the World in 1900, Aleister Crowley was not yet ready to settle down in Boleskine House. Paris beckoned. Paris the City of artists, musicians and dancers and all manner of creative necromancers was a bright glistening jewel across the Channel. Crowley hastened there to complete magical rituals with MacGregor Mathers and inform him of the goings on in the Order of the Golden Dawn, back in London.

But he returned to Boleskine House in February 1900. This was a turbulent time of change for society and a new century of optimism and progress.

Crowley returned to London in April that year in a state of tension. He was almost at War with himself. What tormented him was the accomplishment of the Abra-Melin ritual, versus changes within the Order of the Golden Dawn. This restlessness meant he was neither in one place nor another. He had not completely let go of London, nor was he completely at home and relaxed in Boleskine House. He could not commit to completing a magical ritual he saw as essential and he could not let go of his personal ambitions in the Order of the Golden Dawn - which completing the Abra-Melin would confer on him.

He returned to Blythe Road and entered a battle which he lost, against W B Yeats and the police by demanding entrance to the flat and the Order. MacGregor Mathers, due to this row and drama was also thrown out of the Order of the Golden Dawn and Crowley went again to Paris to report to him on events.

At the suggestion of friends of MacGregor Mathers in Paris, Crowley set sail for Mexico in June 1900, travelling firstly to New York. The battle between settling in Scotland and travelling the World at this time was easily won by Travel and a new found wanderlust. Crowley was a force unleashed. He sought more climbing experience and links with others in the magical fraternity. He sought also to explore, uncover and learn. In July 1900 he landed in New York where he stayed for a few days then journeyed by train to Mexico City.

ALAMEDA PARK, MEXICO

Crowley rented a house there overlooking Alameda Park, notorious for prostitution. He explored both Magick and prostitution with enthusiasm whilst in Mexico City. He then went to Guadalajara in February 1901 with Oscar Eckenstein the climber, who was visiting him. They visited various Mexican Mountain ranges and talked of planning an expedition to the Himalayas.

Guadalajara - Mexico

Crowley then travelled to Hawaii in May 1901 and fell in love there with a married woman called Mary Beaton whom he called 'Alice'. She inspired him to write poetry and he wrote to Gerald Kelly about her. Mary, however returned to her husband after the holiday romance. Crowley journeyed on to San Francisco via El Paso. He liked San Francisco and spent time in the Chinese community there, also burning incense, and meditating at the Buddhist Temple.

San Francisco 1900

Crowley's next visit was to the Orient at this time, and was rather short. He would return again later in his Life. He visited Japan and met up with his friend and fellow Golden Dawn member Elaine Simpson in Hong Kong, and also called in on Ceylon.
There he met up with Allan Bennett in Colombo whose health had improved and who was tutoring the sons of the Solicitor General of Ceylon. Bennett gave up this job and went with Crowley to Kandy where they rented a bungalow in the hills overlooking a lake. Here Bennett taught Crowley yoga and its spiritual wisdom for six weeks and this foundation was the intense basis of his knowledge of Yoga that he would work again with later in his Life.

Crowley now sought to climb Chogo Ri or what is also known as K2, in the Himalayas. He wired Eckenstein on 23rd August about a commitment for an expedition in Spring 1902. In November 1901 Crowley parted with Bennett who went to Burma to take up residence in a Buddhist Monastery. Crowley travelled to India and in Madura donned a loincloth and went begging with his new found knowledge of Yoga. He felt creative in India and wrote poetry and resolved to visit Bennett in Burma. In January 1902 he set sail for Rangoon. There he met up with Bennett again on 14 February 1902 at the Buddhist Monastery. Bennett had a new name Bhikkhu Ananda Sanajotika Metteyya and would later found the International Buddhist Society in Burma in 1903.

I have worked out that Aleister Crowley's best Direction according to his Kua number in Feng Shui was West and of course West was America. Auspicious for

Health was the South West and here I would include areas such as Mexico and New Orleans, North East was best for family and descendants here the UK and Scotland, and the North West for Prosperity which would of course include Boleskine House. The other directions are inauspicious, Chueh Ming being East for Crowley and the area of Total Loss, including that of children, loss of Wealth and bankruptcy and severe and chronic illness. The seeds of his loss were sown during this period in the East. South was the area for Crowley of the Five Ghosts, a location of bad luck, quarrels and misunderstandings, fires and loss of income. We can transfer this 'South' to the South of London in relation to the laws of the Kua. The South East was also inauspicious as was North and the area of Ho Hai or accidents and mishaps such as those which would later befall the fated climb of K2.

The principles of Chinese Magic are contained in the Lo Shu which is the foundation of Taoist magical practice. Many of Taoism's magical rituals are synchronised in accordance with the Lo Shu pattern. The ancient Chinese believed that the Universe was based on mathematical principles. Numbers were the Key to the invisible forces that governed Heaven and Earth. Feng Shui formulas are based on the Lo Shu number grid. The mysterious secrets of the Lo Shu number grid are further revealed when it is placed on the Pa Kua or Feng Shui Compass. Thus numerology, the Lo Shu and the Pa Kua are the cornerstones of Compass School of Feng Shui. Here we have discovered that Aleister Crowley's magic Number is 7. Although in the basic Pa Kua the Number 7 corresponds to East - in the Lo Shu Pa Kua for Aleister Crowley, this direction is inauspicious and his Best Direction is West. Below is the format for the Magic Square or Lo Shu.

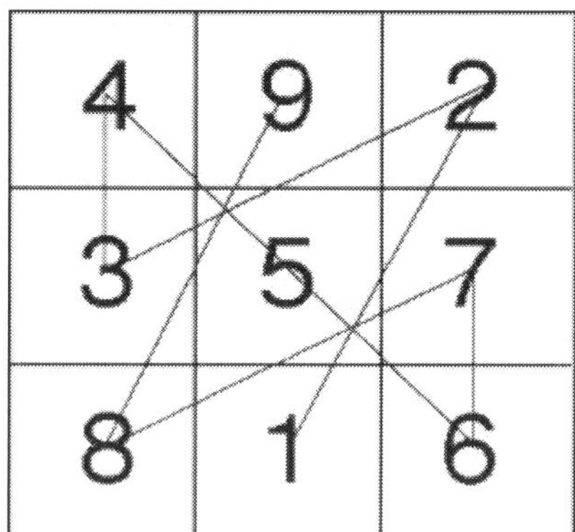

In which ever direction these numbers always add up to 15.
The ancient Hebrew sign for Saturn is similar to the symbol created by the sequence of numbers in the Lo Shu. This is a V of 1,2,3 - a line of 4,5,6 And a backward V of 7,8,9.
In the Feng Shui of individual homes, it is best to use one of the Nine Cures to enhance, strengthen or redirect threatening elements or negative energy. In this book where we are using Compass and Topographical Feng Shui, mostly the negative directions are best avoided, for living or working in.

THE ASCENT OF K2 - DECISIONS & CHANGES IN CROWLEY'S LIFE

In June 1902 Crowley with Eckenstein and their party began their ascent of K2 or Chogo Ri as it is also known. They climbed the South East Ridge and set up camp at 18,773 feet. The weather broke and Eckenstein and Knowles fell ill with 'flu. The weather cleared at the end of June and they set off again.
In July two other climbers with their party managed to climb to a height of 22,000 feet. However when Wesseley and Guillarmod returned they found Crowley ill with Malaria and a temperature of 103 degrees. In his delerium he threated Knowles with a colt revolver. Another member of the group became ill, Pfannl was diagnosed by Crowley as having a pulmonary oedema, which the others thought to be pneumonia. He was treated with morphine and sent back down the mountain. The bad weather got the better of them and they had to abandon the climb. They had to wait until early August to descend. In the village of Skardu they found fresh food again as they were very hungry. In September they arrived in Srinigar but their efforts of endurance to conquer K2 were ignored and not chronicled in the Alpine Club in London. There were no accolades for this brave attempt either in the press or in climbing circles.

In Feng Shui, the Dragon Mountain had overcome and dispersed the would be conquerors. However Crowley as usual was undaunted. He was on to the next leg of his Life journey.

On October 4th Crowley set sail on the SS Egypt for Aden. Leaving from India he journeyed to Cairo for some weeks of relaxation and indulgence. However he arrived in Paris in November 1902 and went to see Macgregor Mathers.

An argument developed about some luggage Crowley had left with Mathers. This argument turned into a dilemma for Crowley. A woman, at Macgregor Mathers apartment tried to seduce Crowley and drain him of energy he later declared. However his energy levels would have been low anyway due to his asthma and malaria. His health prevented him from travelling at this time.

Crowley thus spent the Winter in Montparnasse, in Paris with Gerald Kelly in his studio at Rue Campagne Premier. He wasted no time in getting to know the bohemian hoi poloi such as Nina Oliver, an artists' model, Arnold Bennett, William Somerset Maugham, Clive Bell, Paul Wayland Bartlett and James Wilson Maurice. Writers , artists and sculptors all interested him though Crowley always stood out from the crowd. "It had already been branded on my forehead", he said, "that I was the Spirit of Solitude, the Wanderer of the Waste, Aleister. For while I entered with absolute spontaneous enthusiasm into the artistic atmosphere of Paris, I was always subconsciously aware that here I had no continuing City". He felt branded. Nonetheless he was at this time invited to the sculptor Rodin's studio to see his works as Crowley was a great admirer of Rodin. He also enjoyed himself with witty conversations at the Café Chat Blanc, accompanied by Gerald Kelly and the rest of the bohemian set.

PARIS 1920 - Montparnasse

BOLESKINE BECKONS

Crowley returned to Boleskine House in April 1903. He began to write up his spiritual progress and mystical experiences. He was deciding on his next step after assessing Buddhism, Hinduism and Yoga, and came back to realising that Magic with its drama and intensity was calling him again.

Loch Ness from Boleskine House

Crowley's physical and sexual desires were pressing at this time and his mind turned once again to considering using prostitutes. However In August 1903 he received an invitation from Gerald Kelly which was to change the course of his life. Kelly was staying at Strathpeffer with his mother and his sister Rose. Crowley found Rose engaging. She took Crowley into her confidence and explained that her family were trying to press her into marriage with a man she did not love. Crowley offered her a solution, she could marry him and they would have an open marriage. Being only 27 years old and not having thought matters through clearly, he saw their marriage as a simple solution to Rose's problem. However deep down he probably wished to marry, his proposal offered him the security he craved. So they married on 12 August 1903 in Dingwall. They had both told Gerald Kelly they were off to get married but he took it as a joke and went off to play golf.

Rose Kelly

Rose was the answer to Crowley's prayers, sexual desires and passion. She had been married before to a Major Skerritt and they had lived in South Africa but 2 years after their marriage he had died. She had returned to her family and according to Crowley had inherited alcoholism from her mother. However Rose entranced him in the early years of their marriage. She had a lively, adaptable and adventurous spirit, was well educated and loved to travel.

Crowley wrote of her, "Physically and morally Rose exercised on every man she met a fascination which I have never seen anywhere else, not a fraction of it. She was like a character in a romantic novel, a Helen of Troy or a Cleopatra., yet while more passionate, unhurtful. She was essentially a good woman. Her love sounded every abyss of lust, soared to every splendour of the empyrean" After a few weeks at Boleskine House they began a long honeymoon, starting in Paris.

Crowley and Rose enjoyed themselves in Paris and travelled on through Marseilles and Naples to arrived in Cairo, Egypt in November 1903 where they planned to visit the Pyramids. Crowley and Rose spent the night in the King's Chamber or the Great Pyramid where he performed a ritual by candlelight

Paris 1900

December 1903 found Crowley and Rose arriving in Ceylon. Here Rose told Crowley she had an announcement to make - she was pregnant. Their journey plans changed and they went to Hambantota in South East Ceylon and planned to be back at Boleskine House before the birth of the baby. Whilst on a Hunting Expedition Crowley wrote more poetry and an exquisite love poem to Rose called Rosa Mundi. Rosa Mundi was the Rose of the Rosicrucian Cross and an 'homage' to his wife.

"Rose of the World!
Red glory of the secret heart of Love
Red flame, rose-red, most subtly curled
Into its own infinite flower, all flowers above!
Its flower in its own perfumed passion,
Its faint, sweet passion, folded and furled
In flower fashion
And my deep spirit takes its pure part
Of that voluptuous heart
Of hidden happiness"

Could there be anything which gave evidence to Crowley's deep love for Rose more intensely? Or the 'red-flame....most subtly curled' the sleeping foetus waiting to be born? Interestingly Crowley published these love poems as Rosa Mundi and Other Love Songs by H D Carr - pseudonymously. However travelling back to England meant another call to Cairo where Crowley would dress up as Chioa Khan, an oriental gentleman.

Rose, Crowley & Nuit

Crowley studied Arabic whilst in Cairo and wanted to understand the basics of Islamic Prayer. He consulted a sheikh who also taught him the mysticism and magic of Islam and the secrets of Sidi Aisawa, a Sufi order. On 17 March he performed a ritual invoking the Egyptian God Thoth which he deemed a great success. Rose as Ouarda the Seer revealed to him that Horus too wanted to address him.

Ouarda the Seer, or rather, Rose as a Medium, told Crowley that an emissary of Horus wanted to communicate with him. This emissary was called Aiwass and was to become influential in much magic and ritual Crowley was to perform throughout his life. This was a creative and spiritual time for Crowley and formed much of the basis of his work. He later looked back on and realised that Rose was his first Scarlet Woman "who is any woman that receives and transmits my Solar Word and being - for without Woman, man has no power..." This significant psychic awakening for Crowley was impossible without Rose and was to remain a foundation stone in his writings and magical ritual for the rest of his life.

Crowley left Egypt for Paris with Rose and her growing pregnancy. They arrived in May 1904 and met up with Clive Bell and Arnold Bennett; he also paid a courtesy visit to MacGregor Mathers. Then Aleister and Rose returned to Boleskine House and a summer in 1904 of family joy, of social pleasures and of reading and writing. Even his Aunt, Anne Bishop visited, Gerald Kelly came and the Kelly family's hostility towards the marriage ebbed. Crowley decided to take greater control over his literary works and with the help of Ivor Back, as editor, set to compiling 3 volumes of his written works.

Grounds of Boleskine House

Nuit was born on 28 July 1904 and named Nuit Ma Ahathoor Hecate Sappho Jezebel Lilith Crowley and Crowley waxed lyrical about her through the sum of all her names. He also wrote erotic poems to amuse Rose. Crowley enjoyed family life over the Summer and went to St Moritz in Switzerland in October 1904. Rose and the baby followed in the November. This was a short break and they returned to Boleskine for the Winter. Rose feared that she was once again pregnant and sought the advice of a nurse for a termination. The Nurse clumsily poisoned her with ergot. Crowley was away at this time and returned to find his wife very ill. The reason for this illness caused a deep rift in the marriage because Crowley was completely opposed to abortion. Gradually Rose recovered and the Nurse was dismissed. Rose had not been pregnant at all.
In April 1905 Crowleys' friend Dr Jacot Guillarmod who he knew from the K2 expedition in 1902, visited Boleskine House. He proposed a new expedition to

Kanchenjunga, the third highest mountain in the World, also in the Himalayas. It was considered to be an even greater challenge than Everest. Although Crowley insisted on leading this Expedition though his leadership was sadly lacking. Eckenstein, Crowley's old friend and mountaineer judged the risks to be too great & said as much to Gerald Kelly. He did not go. Crowley asked Knowles to come with them, who he'd previously threatened. Knowles wisely declined. So Crowley asked Guillarmod, a mediocre climber to help create the team. Such a journey is usually planned over a couple of years. However they planned to make an assault on Kanchenjunga that same year. They left for Calcutta in the May and arrived in Darjeeling in the August, 1902.

Calcutta

This expedition was ill fated and a failure. There was disagreement between Crowley and Guillarmod and porters deserted them. One porter died and his death was seen by the other porters as a sacrifice to the god of Kanchenjunga. Porters claimed to Guillarmod that Crowley had beaten them and Guillarmod then decided with de Righi to depose Crowley and take charge of the expedition. Thus Guillarmod seized leadership with de Righi and Pache and Crowley and Redmond became a second camp. However an accident caused the death of Pache and 3 more porters. Crowley heard their cries and sent out Redmond to help but did not help himself. He later descended Kanchenjunga and never again returned to the Himalayas. This time was the beginning of his bad reputation in the press via the Daily Mail and through the British Alpine Club who turned against him. Crowley, being Crowley could not admit that he had done anything wrong.

Kanchenjunga

A TURNING POINT

By October 1905 Crowley was 30. His marriage was in tatters and he had not achieved the greatness he felt he deserved either in Literary circles or in the field of Mountaineering. He journeyed to Calcutta and at this time worked on his poetry and in particular 'The Scented Garden of Abdullah' and 'Gargoyles'.

Calcutta

However this was a period of introspection and he wrote of himself;
"I realise in myself the perfect impossibility of reason. Suffering great misery I am as one who should have plumed himself for years upon the speed and strength of a favourite horse, only to find that its speed and strength were illusory, but that it was not a real horse at all, but a clothes-horse".

In fact Crowley was a Pig or Boar, according to Chinese Astrology. There are 12 animals in Chinese Astrology and the Pig became an animal Sign in an unusual way. In ancient times there was a rich Senior Officer who had no sons. He was desperate to carry on his family line and offered many prayers and sacrifices to the Gods. Finally at the age of 60 he had a son. In celebration he held a party and invited fortune-tellers who unanimously told him that his son had a promising future. However, the boy's parents spoiled him and he grew selfish and pampered, and after his father's death he sold off the family fortune to support his lifestyle. Eventually he ran out of money, his friends deserted him, and he died in poverty and misery soon afterwards.
Upon arriving in Hell after his death, he complained to the Jade Emperor in Heaven that he had been unfairly deprived of his promising fate. After further enquiry the Emperor decided that although the man had been born with a good destiny, he had squandered it. The Emperor punished him by ordering that he be reborn a pig, 'feeding upon the chaff'. However the heavenly officer in charge, misheard this, as 'becoming an animal sign' which sounds very similar in Chinese. As a result that man was reborn not only as a pig, but also as an animal sign.

The reader may notice a small similarity between this story and the Feng Shui journey of Mr Aleister Crowley. Whilst in Calcutta Crowley was ambushed or mugged as we would say today. He used a pistol to defend himself and shot the attacker. This matter was not reported to the police and once Rose and Nuit arrived at the end of October they set sail immediately for Rangoon to visit Allan Bennett, now called Ananda Metteyya and a Buddhist Monk, in some haste. Once there, Rose and Nuit were to stay at an hotel and Crowley journeyed alone to see Ananda Metteyya. Here Perdurabo spent time in contemplation and reflection upon his own Karma. Had he killed a man?

Crowley spent time meditating on his own karma with Ananda Metteyya. He followed the meditative techniques that he later used in Magic. He consciously reversed the order of Time by remembering the events of his Life in reverse sequence. This meant that ultimately he could delve into past lives.
From this spiritual sojourn he returned to Rangoon where Rose and his daughter waited.
There he decided to explore Burma and its border region with Southern China. This region was unexplored by white people at the time and he was advised to leave his family behind by a British diplomat. He ignored this advice.

Crowley and Rose took a steamship along the Irrawaddy River on 15 November 1905. In December they crossed into China. On the way Crowley fell with his horse from a cliff for 40 feet, yet he luckily emerged unharmed. He again felt a strong sense of purpose to his Life, and felt the Holy Guardian Angel of the Abra-melin had saved him. Fate was pointing the direction he should travel in.

In January 1906 they reached Tengchong, and met up with the British Consul, Litton who offered Crowley travel advice which he took. Crowley noted from this time " For the first time in my Life I was really free...I found myself in the middle of China with a wife and child...there was a man,
Aleister Crowley, husband and father........and it was his business to give them His undivided love, care and protection........." He decided that he would try to perform the Abra-melin, whilst travelling and without a quiet temple setting.

In China Crowley learned of the I Ching and the Tao Te Ching and felt a strong connection to the pulse of oriental Life and the mysteries of the Orient.

Temple of the Cave Dragon - China

In March Crowley left Yannanfu and journeyed south to Vietnam. He had fallen out with his Chinese porters and quarrelled with Rose. They hired a dugout and travelled down the red River to Hokow. From there they went to Hanoi and took a ship for Hong Kong. In Hong Kong Rose returned to India to pick up some remaining luggage and then left for the UK via the Suez Canal and the Mediterranean. Crowley had other plans. He was to go to Japan and then on to Canada and North America via the Pacific. He had plans to try to elicit support for another Kanchenjunga expedition, in New York.

However first he went to Shanghai to visit Elaine Simpson to whom he now felt attracted. Her membership of the Golden Dawn was also an attraction. He discussed 'The Book of the Law' with her but they did not become lovers due to his respect for her, or perhaps his marriage. Crowley left for Japan on 21 April. He performed an Invocation there that elevated him magically and continued his magical workings as he travelled. In May 1906 he travelled from Vancouver to New York and as he crossed the continent he worked on his invocation daily. From New York he left for Liverpool arriving there on 2nd June 1906.

TRAVEL - A HOUSE OF LOSS

Travel and Long Journeys are in the House of the North according to the Feng Shui Compass and the 8 Aspirations. This for Crowley was a house of Loss and Disaster, being a number 7. Travel slowly leaked away his finances and resources throughout his life. If only he had remained at Boleskine and continued his writing and magical work. If... Of the Feng Shui Masters I have studied North was for Man-Ho Kwok, Disaster and for Wu Xing, Disagreement. I would add that 7 is not to be confused with Crowley's Chinese Astrology Number which I will go into later.

Crowley arrived in Liverpool to find 2 letters. The first told him that his daughter Nuit had died in Rangoon of Typhoid. She was not yet 2 years old.
The second letter told Crowley that his wife Rose had retreated into grief and alcoholism. Yet she was pregnant again. Crowley was bereaved. He tried to make sense of the death by looking at the spiritual Path he was on. He did reunite with Rose but both were shaken to the point of illness due to their grief; they again parted.

To push his thoughts away from this and begin something new he talked with George Cecil Jones about forming a new magical order. In late summer Rose gave birth to Lola Zaza who was born as a sickly infant. Oxygen provided at birth by Crowley helped to revive her and a ritual was performed to give thanks for her birth. Crowley felt able to begin new things again in the autumn, and in October 1906 considered that he had finished the Abra-melin Operation. He became rootless again and was spending time in London, Eastbourne and Bournemouth alternatively by December 1906. His attempts at marriage and family life were in tatters. He did by now understand, however that all attainment is predestined by Karma. He was smoking much hashish at this time to step into a new form of consciousness, and to try to differentiate drugged illusions from Samadhi. Yet he had barely acknowledged his grief.

Captain John Frederick Charles Fuller

Crowley began his new magical order the A:.A:. with George Cecil Jones and later a new member Captain John Frederick Charles Fuller. He parted from Rose and his daughter and rented a flat. He had various lovers including Ada Leverson and Vera Snepp. Here he bought what ever drugs he needed from a Chemists shop in Stafford Street run by E P Whineray. He took on the Earl of Tankerville as a magical student. Crowley insisted that they take on a Great Magical Retirement which was to be a journey via Paris to Marseilles then Gibraltar and Morocco. Tankerville, a naïve young man, was unhappy in Morocco and insisted on returning to England in July 1907. Crowley at this time became creatively productive and through his Spiritual Guides received two books - the Book of Lapis Lazuli and - The Book of the Heart Girt with a Serpent. He also wrote a satiric drama, The World's Tragedy. It was also at this time that he met with Victor Neuberg in the Spring of 1908. Neuberg had also studied at Trinity in Cambridge and was publishing poems in The Agnostic Journal, and had a poetry book published called The Green Garland. Their attraction was immediate and we can say that Neuberg fell in love with Crowley, whilst Crowley, the teacher was a confidante and guide. Crowley had moved out of 21 Warwick Road, Kensington for good.

Crowley journeyed again to Paris in January 1908 and stayed there until the April at 50 Rue Vavin.

When he returned to London in June 1908 he hired a Doctor Leslie W Murray to treat Rose and get her to employ a nanny for Lola Zaza. She was in a bad way and her drinking had deteriorated her character and temperament. Crowley again returned to Paris in the July, and Victor Neuberg came to join him as soon as the Summer Term had ended in Cambridge. At this time he had taken a new lover Euphemia Lamb the wife of the artist Henry Lamb. She had often sat as a model for Augustus John. Neuberg was stunned at Crowley's relationship with Euphemia, a woman he also was attracted to. Yet he was the lover of Crowley, the arrangement was disturbing to him.

Neuberg the student obeyed his master and followed fasts and rituals as instructed by Crowley at this time. To continue their magical journey together they went to Spain and Morroco and were there during September 1908. Neuberg was undoubtedly in love with Crowley at this time and in his later poetry gives him the name Olivia Vane. Neuberg writes, "Sweet Wizard, in whose footsteps I have trod, Unto the shrine of the most obscene God.......Oh thou who has sucked my soul, Lord of my Nights and Days, My body pure and whole is merged within the ways that lead to thee, My Queen..........." Some of those Rituals Crowley and Neuberg performed are described by Richard Cavendish in his work 'The Black Arts'. Their courage and daring was great and their sexual relationship intense.

MORROCO

Yet Crowley returned to Paris alone, and Neuberg to London. He began a Magical Retirement in October 1908. He was slipping into earthly indulgences and noted "I am so far from The Path that I have a real good mind to get Mary T to let me perform the Black Mass at Midnight on her........" Yet Crowley's birthday the 12th October came and he found a new perception with the recital of another holy book , the Liber Ararita. Paris remained the creative escape it had always been for him. He read Somerset Maughams' novel 'The Magician' whilst there and relished the character Oliver Haddo, based upon himself.
He noted, "Maugham had taken some of the most private and personal incidents of my life...He had added a number of absurd legends.....I was not in the least offended by the attempts of the book to represent me, in many ways as the most atrocious scoundrel, for he had done more than justice, to the qualities of which I was proud..........".'The Magician' was in fact an appreciation of my genius, such as I had never dreamed of inspiring".
Crowley's creativity expanded and the idea grew to launch 'The Equinox' , a journal and his New Order. Paris at this time was a cauldron for his growing magical movement and followers in 1908.

FENG SHUI AND THE ALEISTER CROWLEY JOURNEY

Understanding Energy, from the Earth beneath us or the Skies above us is fundamental to Feng Shui. The impact of Energy on the lives of individuals Is also vital. Energy such as beneficial Chi - the positive energy we wish to direct into our homes or our lives. Energy such as Wind and Water which announce the practice of Feng Shui. For Aleister Crowley the restless Feng Shui Journey in his life dissipated energy. Throughout his travelling one can feel the drip-drip effect of a leaking tap. The beneficial Chi is seeping away and with it Money, Good Friends, Children, Beneficial and Influential people, Relatives, Unfinished Work, Unsubstantiated Theories, incomplete Rituals, Jettisoned friendships and more. In Feng Shui we need to understand the 5 Elements and their Constructive and Destructive Cycles. It is a form of Magic, to gain control of these elements in our Lives, in our homes, in our work and on our Journey.

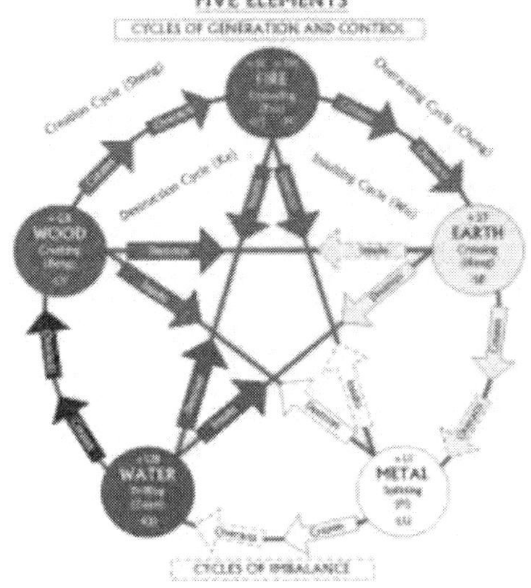

The Control Cycle is as follows:- Fire controls Metal. If Fire is too Powerful Metal loses its power.
Earth controls Water. If Earth is too powerful it impedes the natural flow of Water.
Metal controls Wood. If Metal is overpowering, it may harm Wood.
Water controls Fire. If Water is too forceful it may extinguish Fire.
Wood controls Earth. If Wood is too expansive it disturbs Earth energy.
Basic to Feng Shui is Yin and Yang, harmony and balance in all things.
The Cycle of Imbalance is the reverse of this.
The Feng Shui Master must also understand the I Ching or The Book of Changes which Crowley began to understand and use later in his Life. It determines the likely flow of Events. The trigrams of the I Ching are the Trigrams of the Pa Kua, the Feng Shui Compass. Because Crowley was a number 7 his best directions were North East, North West, West and South West. The Trigrams for these directions are Ken, Mountain, Steadiness/Stillness - Ch'ien, heaven, creative and strong, father - Tui, Lake, Joy and Serenity, Youngest Daughter and K'un Earth, receptive and yielding, Mother. It can be

seen now that these areas and elements were greatly beneficial to Crowley's

life and needed Time, attention and nurturing.
These directions offered
West - Life and Good Fortune
North East - Longevity and Vitality
North West - Vitality and Longevity
South West - Life and Good Fortune
The Unlucky Directions were:
North, K'an, Water - danger, flowing water, Son
South , Li, Fire, adherence, dependence, middle daughter
South East, Sun, Wind, Penetration, Gentleness, eldest daughter
East - Chen, Thunder, Arousing Movement, Eldest Son
These directions brought:-
North - Disaster
South - Five Ghosts
East - Death
South East - Unlucky Influences.

I am reminded of the deaths of Crowley's daughter, the assailant in China, the Deaths in the Himalayas. The 5 ghosts are departed spirits of people who once lived on earth. This direction will have a haunted feeling to it, whether in a home or the area or country once visited. The area of Disaster is an area of accidents and physical injury.

North, in the Pa Kua is traditionally the direction of career and long journeys. With such a Feng Shui Pa Kua it would have benefited Crowley to practice, perform and write of his Magic at Boleskine House in Scotland. When travelling his best direction was West to America. But it would be some time before he would realise this, and most of his money would have been sifted away like sand through his fingers.

BOLESKINE ONCE MORE

BOLESKINE HOUSE TODAY

It was in June 1909 that Crowley returned to Boleskine House on the banks of Loch Ness with Victor Neuberg and Kenneth Ward. Here he rediscovered the manuscript of The Book of the Law on which he decided to start work again. Victor Neuberg, as his student, completed a 10 day magical retirement at Boleskine. Neuberg had taken a Vow of Obedience to Crowley when they were in Morroco in 1908. The training was hard though and at times abusive and Spartan. For example he was made to sit out all night in the damp, cold air. It affected his health for the rest of his life and he recalled in detail this time to his biographer, Jean Overton Fuller, in her book on his life 'The Magical Dilemma of Victor Neuberg'.

Crowley and Rose decided at this time to divorce, and this was filed in Scotland, with adultery as the grounds. The hearing was on 24 November 1909. Rose was still at 21 Warwick Road, Kensington. She was awarded guardianship of Lola Zaza and £52 annually. A £4000 trust fund was set up for Lola Zaza. Two years later in Autumn 1911 Rose was committed by Crowley to Colney Hatch Mental Hospital, later known as Friern Barnet Hospital, in North London for alcoholism dementia. Eventually she recovered and remarried.

Colney Hatch Mental Hospital, North London

It was in November 1909 that Crowley and Neuberg travelled to Algeria to perform Enochian Magic. Crowley shaved Neuberg's head save for two tufts to resemble horns. They undertook a long desert trek to the Oasis of Bou Saada. Crowley wore a turban and grew a beard. Sometimes he led Neuberg about on a leash. In a rite of Pan ritual a magical sexual act occurred. Again I would refer the reader to Richard Cavendish's work, 'The Black Arts' for a further view of this Enochian Magic.

Bou Saada Oasis, Algeria

After completing this magical sojourn Crowley and Neuberg returned to England on 31 December 1909. They returned to the new London flat he had rented at 124 Victoria Street in Central London. Here bohemia reined, and this flat became a place of gathering where drink, drugs, open views and love affairs were tolerated. Whilst still with Neuberg, Crowley also became involved with Betty Bickers. Married, Betty was a name amongst other lovers such as Maisie Clarke or Margot Cripps. Was he bisexual? Or were these women a front for his homosexuality at this time? Possibly, though we see that by now Crowley had certainly overcome the boundary that is Sexuality. It was in 1910 that Crowley met Leila Waddell an Australian musician of part-Maori ancestry. She was a violinist and great beauty. Crowley and Leila became lovers and she was ordained a member of the A:.A:. in April 1910. Other members who joined the order at this time were the poet Meredith Starr, Naval Commander G M Marston, Psychic Researcher Everard Fielding, and the artist Austin Osman Spare. The Equinox was published and also works of poetry such as, Ambergris, The Winged Beetle and also 'the Scented Garden'. Neuberg published 'The Triumph of Pan' about their walk through Spain in 1908. Crowley had created for himself the Magical and Bohemian circle he had dreamed of in Paris. He reviewed 'The Triumph of Pan' a book of poems by Victor Neuberg, in The Equinox, in a playful and positive way. Crowley was later described in a novel by Ethel Archer from this time; 'The Heiroglyph'. She outlines in some detail his flat at 124 Victoria Street.

LEILA WADDELL

It was at 124 Victoria Street that Crowley chose to perform many magical Rituals and in particular The Rites of Eleusis. This is a dramatic ritual about the goddess Demeter seeking out her daughter Persephone who has been abducted by Hades and taken to the Underworld. Major players in these rituals apart from Crowley himself were Victor Neuberg and Crowley's new Scarlet Woman, Leila Waddell. In November and December 1910 the Rites of Eleusis were performed at Caxton Hall.

Caxton Hall

It was at this time and in the South West of London that Aleister Crowley encountered personal slurs and character attacks. Although this is an area of Good Luck for Crowley according to the Pa Kua, we can say that 124 Victoria Street, faces the South and an area of Loss for him. On December 17th 1910 he and Neuberg left England for Algeria and another Sahara trek. Though this trip was a sexually active one between Crowley and Neuberg it was devoid of the true spark of Magic, they had experienced in past sojourns. It was also the demise of their relationship and the cause of them parting.

Algerian Desert

Crowley returned to London and to a defamation trial in April 1911. His friendship with Captain Fuller collapsed after this and his magical order the A:.A:. As usual he took off for Paris and spent the Summer there in 1911, at a Pied-a-terre at 50 Rue Vavin.

PARIS 1910

Pied a Terre at Rue Vavin, Paris - built 1912

It was at 50 Rue Vavin that Crowley launched himself into a frenzy of writing. He wrote poems and short stories, and nineteen essays, perhaps inspired by the prolific Somerset Maugham. He also began his 'Confessions' in which he outlined his work on sexual magic. His theory was to work on alchemical symbols in sexual terms. Ultimately he believed it was possible to create the 'Philosopher's Stone'. Leila Waddell was Crowley's companion and lover at this time, though she could not, in the end, commit to Magic. Finally in October he settled on a new lover Mary Desti, a friend of Isadora Duncan.

Mary Desti

Crowley met Mary Desti at the Savoy Hotel on her birthday the 11th October, the day before his own. She was 40 and he 36, both Librans, and they became lovers. Crowley also showed his natural rebellious streak this year in Paris. Jacob Epstein the sculptor had created a statue for Oscar Wilde's grave in Paris which showed a bare penis. The authorities had covered this with tarpaulin. Crowley announced that he would remove the tarpaulin on 5th November. This he did with no opposition, and few onlookers, on a dull rainy day. However he gained press coverage in both London and Paris, to his delight.

Mary Desti became Crowley's new Scarlett Woman that November and they travelled to St Moritz for a Winter holiday. She proved to be a 'seer' of sorts and brought forth spiritual workings which resulted in Book 4; from her Spirit Guide called Abuldiz. In January the lovers travelled to Italy, to Naples to complete more magical workings.

Naples 1912

Though Mary Desti divorced her husband Solomon Sturges, she did not marry Crowley who she later quarrelled with and left. She then married a Turkish man Veli Bey. Crowley and Mary made up and remained friends and she became an editor of 'The Equinox' during 1913. Their work 'Book 4' is a significant Piece of writing and adds to his early writings on Magick. Part one concerns Meditation. Part 2 describes Ceremonial Magic. The Book of Lies was written around this time in 1913 and combines both Poetry and Magic.
May 1912, found Crowley living in the Avenue Studios off the Fulham Road in London, a neighbour of John Singer Sargeant, the painter. Here he received a visit from Theodore Reuss of the O T O who accused him of violating the honour of the OTO. His, 'Book of Lies' was not published until 1913 so dates are hazy on this matter. However, the revelation of sexual magic was at issue here. Reuss felt some part of the 'Book of Lies' had revealed secrets which should have been kept. Crowley was initially unsure of what he was referring to. Reuss had given Crowley the task of rewriting the OTO rituals when he was originally welcomed into the OTO. They were closely based on Freemasonry. Reuss felt Crowley had transgressed, though after talks and discussions matters were ironed out.

Avenue Studios

Crowley had used the OTO as a means of spreading the word of Thelema his new doctrine.

During this time he met Vittoria Cremers, a dark occultist figure, who he asked to manage the property of the Mysteria, Mystica, Maxima. Cremers knew of a Robert Donston who she claimed, to Crowley, was Jack the Ripper. Donston died in 1912 but was a love rival to Mabel Collins who Vittoria Cremers desired. Crowley weaved this tale into his Confessions and it is the basis of his link to Jack the Ripper. Crowley's hedonism and desire for influencing others is also evident when meeting the writer Katherine Mansfield around this time. He introduced her to peyote or hashish and her subsequent rapturous experience was included in some of her writing.

During the Autumn of 1913 Crowley shaved his head and had his photo taken for the cover of The Equinox Vol I No10. He began to refer to himself as 'the demon Crowley' in the third person. Certainly the drugs he used were beginning to deteriorate his character and nature.

It was in August 1912, that Joan Hayes known also as Ione de Forest, shot herself. She was the lover of Victor Neuberg and Crowley did not approve of their liaison. Joan married Wilfred Merton but continued her affair with Neuberg who was devastated by her death. Neuberg was convinced that Crowley had murdered her through psychological bullying, or magical means.

An ultimate act of jealousy and betrayal, it may have been true. Neuberg lost interest in Crowley and Magic at this time, as Jean Overton Fuller described in her work 'The Magical Dilemma of Victor Neuberg', and felt a fear and loathing of Crowley for many years.

This period of time in London was an important one for Crowley in terms of the influential people he met and his magical contacts. He was still relatively young, 38 in 1913, and attractive to women. Crowley and Neubergs' relationship was at an end and as a diversion he travelled with Leila Waddell to Russia where she was performing on stage in The Ragged Ragtime Girls. Their sexual relationship too had diminished and he began a new sexual liaison in Russia with Anny Ringler, a Hungarian woman he met there.

Russian Theatre

These were heady days in Russia. Crowley saw Anny daily but also wrote a lot of poetry. This was a time of change in Russia, for the Russian Revolution was getting underway; and must have influenced his writing particularly, his poem 'Hymn to Pan' which was read at his funeral. Crowley and the Ragged Ragtime Girls returned to London in the Autumn of 1913. He went again to Paris in the December. There he decided to embark on a new series of magical workings . Thus he asked Victor Neuberg to assist him with these and, whether reluctantly or not, Neuberg agreed. From this time on he would devote himself to sexual as opposed to ceremonial magic. Crowley and Neuberg began this work at midnight as 1914 began and through ritual sex, Crowley passive and Neuberg playing the active role. Motivation played its part; it was not a great success.

Paris - Pre World War I

Crowley returned to London and put his personal concerns into the hands of an OTO member called George M Cowie who he met in June 1914. He had mortgaged Boleskine House and now he put it up for lease. Cowie was also to look after Crowley's publishing works. Neuberg and Crowley's relationship was changed completely. Crowley and Neuberg met in London in September or

October 1914 and Neuberg told Crowley he no longer wanted to be Crowley's Disciple.

Victor Neuberg

Crowley was furious and cursed Neuberg. This was probably by nature a quarrel from which Crowley felt betrayed. Neuberg's fear of Crowley may well have been exaggerated. However he had a nervous breakdown and spent time recovering with his Mother in Hove, Sussex. It took him two years to feel well again..

The First World War had begun on 28 July 1914. Crowley offered his services to the British Government on behalf of the War effort. These were rejected due to his phlebitis and his negative character and persona. He made a new positive decision perhaps due to his relationship with Neuberg ending and his marriage over. He would go to America. On 24 October 1914 he boarded the Lusitania for New York. Paris could no longer be his bolt hole due to the War but the New World beckoned.

The Lusitania arriving in New York

THE WESTERN LIFE - A RETREAT FROM STRUGGLE

New York - 1910

Now Crowley had begun to embrace the Western Life which the Pa Kua informs us was his most beneficial direction. West - Trigram Tui, North West, Trigram, Ch'ien and South West, Trigram K'un. These represent Lake, Heaven and Earth - a good balance of energies.

I CHING TRIGRAMS

West	North West	South West
— — _____ _____	____ ____ ____	— — __ __ — —
Lake, Joy, Serenity Youngest Daughter	Heaven Creative, Strong Father	Earth Receptive, Yielding Mother

Certainly the best balance of energies for Aleister Crowley was in America Where he would be able to find peace to be creative. Where there would also be reflection on the past, on his parents and his youngest daughter who had cruelly passed away.

So from the Trigram, Tui for West we see the season Autumn being particularly beneficial. Tui represents the youngest daughter but it also represents mistresses! Here we see the inner psychic world and World of Magick becoming even more important. There is also a need to live in harmony with Nature.

From the Trigram Ch'ien we feel Yang, masculine energy. Its animals are the horse, lion and tiger. Drive and energy, power and strength, logic and courage are here too. Career, creativity and writing come to the fore, swimming, walking and activities linked to others. There is a need for like minded people and to lead by example.
From the Trigram, K'un we feel feminine, Yin energy. Here there is care, nurturing and consideration for others. The influences of women are great. K'un links to the Mother and the Moon, it is also the Earth as endless provider. There is a real sense of Crowley coming together within himself during this time.

The I Ching or Book of Changes is an ancient Oracle that Crowley, later in his Life consulted on a daily basis. It is over 3000 years old. It has an elusive magic which offers profound wisdom. It contains 64 hexagrams. Each hexagram contains 2 trigrams of the Feng Shui Pa Kua. Each trigram contains lines which are either Yin or Yang. Thus the I Ching when consulted will offer a balanced reading. The I Ching is consulted using either 6 wands or 3 ancient Chinese coins for prediction and divination.
Confucius wrote of the I Ching, "The Sage gazes up and contemplates the phenomena of the heavens, then looks down and examines the patterns of the earth; thereby he learns the causes of darkness and light. He traces things to their beginning and follows them to their end, therefore he knows the Significance of Life and Death……"

Crowley's initial contacts in America proved unhelpful. He was cast aside by the wealthy lawyer and arts patron John Quinn who wrote scathingly of him to Yeats and Ezra Pound. Pound writing in The Little Review in 1917 even criticised a positive mention of Crowley by H L Mencken. Crowley wrote an essay called 'The Revival of Magick' which he hoped would draw to him students both male and female in order to perform rituals. In 1915 he became 40 and at this stage of his life was looking for a new Scarlet Woman. However it was in January 1915 that he met George Sylvester Viereck a writer and editor who was supporting the Germans in World War One. He had set up two journals; 'The International' and 'The Fatherland'. Crowley was to write for both of these 2 journals and thereby create his wartime livelihood from 1915 to 1917.

Crowley had met Viereck before in London and renewed his acquaintance with him in New York.
'The Fatherland' was a journal supported by the German Government. Crowley wrote his first article for them entitled 'Honesty is the Best Policy' addressed to the British Government and criticising British Hypocrisy. In taking on such a public statement he was considered by many to be a traitor to the British cause. This was so typical of Crowley! For some reason he also claimed Irish ancestry which also was totally false. Crowley was later to be seen as a small time traitor by Admiral Sir Guy Gaunt, Head of Naval Intelligence during WWI. However, he did make a positive link with British Intelligence at this time, with Everard Fielding. Everard passed on Crowley's desire to be helpful to British Intelligence but they did not completely trust him. Crowley was a wild card, a loose cannon, and unlikely to take orders from others.

In June 1915 he fell in love with Jeanne Foster a New York Beauty and model. Foster was married but embraced occultism and Crowley enthusiastically; she was entranced. Jeanne Foster introduced Crowley to her friend the journalist Helen Hollis and he had affairs with both women. He decided to take a trip to the West Coast of America in October 1915. There Crowley wanted to see how the North American Chapter of the OTO was getting on. He travelled with Foster and her husband by train and on the way they stopped off at Detroit.

Jeanne Foster - Hilarion

Crowley spent his 40th birthday on board the train to the West Coast and spent time in meditation whilst travelling. He felt he was at last a Magus and his name became 'To Mega Therion' or The Great Beast, and Foster was to become his new Scarlet Woman. He composed new poems to her in a book' The Golden Rose' and also wanted her to become pregnant. This did not happen.

They paid a visit to Charles Robert Stansfeld Jones in the Vancouver OTO.

Charles Robert Stansfeld Jones and Wife

Jones was a loyal and devoted disciple of Crowley and had joined the A:.A:. in 1909. His magical name was Frater Achad. He was an intellectually gifted magician and had created a huge circular diagram which completely linked the Tarot with Astrology and the Paths of the Kabbalah. A copy of this unique diagram is in the papers left to Gerald Yorke by Crowley which are in the Warburg Institute. Jones had risen in the ranks of the OTO and became Grand Master for North America in 1921. Crowley was pleased with the Temple Jones and his colleagues had created.

However He and Jeanne Foster fell out and she returned to New York. She made it clear her affair with him was over when he eventually returned to New York and saw her.

There was much animosity between them for quite some time.

Crowley did, however, manage to have another affair with Alice Richardson a singer and wife of Ananda K Coomaraswamy. She performed sex magic with him for a time. However he had also begun an affair with a german prostitute Gerda Maria von Kothek, a lustful woman. Coomaraswamy took his wife away from Crowley when she became pregnant and put her on a ship to England in the Summer of 1916. However she had a miscarriage due to her sea sickness. Crowley was greatly wounded. He blamed her husband for allowing her to sail, yet he had done nothing to stop her going.

It was now June 1916 and Crowley's fortunes had not greatly improved. He decided the Time had come for a great Magical Retirement. The person he turned to for assistance was the accomplished Astrologer, Evangeline Adams.

LAKE PASQUANEY, NEW HAMPSHIRE

Echoes of Boleskine House must have floated through Crowley's mind as he rested and wrote at Evangeline's cottage on Lake Pasquaney, Bristol, New Hampshire. In this beautiful place he stayed for 4 months. Crowley was hired by Evangeline to ghost-write two books on Astrology published under her name -'Astrology - Your Place in the Sun' and also 'Astrology - Your place among the Stars'. Crowley had a growing interest in Astrology and worked away. He had need of the money too. This was the perfect role for him at this time and he continued at her cottage from June until October 1916. There he performed magical rituals and was unrestrained in his use of drugs at this time. Later that summer he had a telegram from Jones in Vancouver to say that Jones had now emerged as Master of the Temple. Crowley was delighted for him and now considered him as his Magical Son. He confirmed him in this new grade.

In October Crowley returned to New York where he had few work prospects save writing for 'The Fatherland'. So in December that year he decided to travel to New Orleans. He there planned to renew his friendship with a Professor Keasbey at the University of Texas. He had met the Professor at Lake Pasquaney in the September. However their friendship was short lived and they disagreed and fell out. Yet Crowley remained in New Orleans during the Winter months of 1917 when he wrote copiously and had doubts over his magical direction.

FRENCH QUARTER - NEW ORLEANS

CHINESE ASTROLOGY & THE YEAR OF THE PIG 1875

1875, the year of Crowley's birth was Yi Hai year, the Year of the Pig passing By. We see here a person honest and straightforward in his opinions but with an outspoken approach which challenges older members of the family. This individual will seek others who share his views. Problems with family will ease as he ages. His year is No12 in the 60 Year cycle. This is the Number of the Wood Pig whose season is early winter and whose colour is green. He was born in the Hour of the Rat, making him hot tempered and someone who dives into situations without much forethought. He is a target for gossip. Only Aging and Time make him more level headed. He will work independently and receive support from family.

Interestingly the day of Birth - 12th creates an individual sensitive to the world around him. There is a disciplined approach to work and a head for business though this is very competitive. People are wary of approaching him because they see him as stern or difficult. Those who know him well know his natural concern for others. The Month of Birth shows someone able to create long lasting friendships. However this is someone strongly opinionated with a resolute Nature. Advice from others helps to avoid the negative effects of his actions; when taken! Later in March, Crowley had bad news from George Cowie the OTO Treasurer in London. Police had raided the OTO London Headquarters due to his articles in 'The Fatherland' and the membership had dwindled. On 6th April 1917 the United States declared War on Germany. Yet Crowley continued to write for Viereck for the money and to express his Work, he said.

When he returned to New York he had another piece of bad news. His Mother, Emily had died. He wrote of his grief in his diary, "I had news of my Mother's death. Two nights before this news, I had a dream that she was dead, and felt very distressed. This very same thing happened before I had news of my Father's death. I had often dreamed that my Mother had died, but never with that helpless, lonely feeling". Emily had left the majority of her estate in Trust for Crowley's ex-wife Rose and for her grand-daughter, Lola-ZaZa. Crowley received an annual sum of £300, but this was to be doled out weekly. It was a financial buffer for him and he 'made do' with it.

In July 1917 Veireck made Crowley the Assistant Editor of 'The International', An avant-garde Arts journal. Crowley worked for $20 a week and filled the pages with much of his writing - which kept contributors costs low. Naturally he had a range of pseudonyms for his contributions. He wrote poems, essays on Magick, and fiction. In October 1917 he moved to an apartment on West 9th Street. He had two lovers around this time Anne Catherine Miller and Roddie Minor who he called 'The Camel' - Minor became his new Scarlet Woman. Crowley also had a homosexual relationship with an African American friend of Minor, Walter Gray a Musician. Roddie became a Seer who was the Medium for Amalantrah, her guide. Walter took part in these invocations too. Some 20 years hence in his tarot card 'The Lovers' a Union of two people, black and white, male and female, seek one another. Crowley knew that Race could be no boundary to Love.

Apartments at West 9th Street New York

Roddie Minor was his Scarlet Women up to March 1918. At one point Crowley wanted to marry her. His interest in her waned when his head was turned by Eva Tanguay. They briefly became lovers though she was also involved with the African American heavyweight Champion Jack Johnson. Crowley was unable to stick with any one woman in America, at this time in his life.
'The International' was sold to Professor Keasbey with whom Crowley had quarrelled. Crowley was expelled from the offices and lost his salary. He did however manage to pen another book at this time, 'Liber Aleph, the Book of Wisdom or Folly'. Crowleys' affair with Roddie Minor came to an end in the Summer of 1918. He decided to take another Great Magical Retirement. This time to Esopus Island, on the Hudson River in Dutchess County. Crowley was paddled there by the journalist William Seabrook, in a canoe.

ESOPUS ISLAND ON THE HUDSON RIVER

Though his finances had improved marginally one could not say, by any stretch of the imagination, that they were adequate. Crowley still lived an aristocratic lifestyle even though he was of modest means. Since leaving Cambridge University he had given no though to money when deciding to travel the World, plan mountaineering ventures, become a writer and poet, and perform magical rituals. It was his Mother Emily who saw through the smoke-screen of glamour and intrigue Crowley created for himself. Perhaps she sought to educate him one last time when she left him merely £300 per annum in her will, and the rest to her ex-daughter-in-law and grand-daughter. Crowley surely must have mused on some of this whilst in isolation, and with little food on Esopus Island. Crowley took only a tin of red paint with him to the Island. Luckily he was visited by Roddie Minor the first weekend who took him some food. He became perhaps the first Graffitti artist locally and painted 'Do What Thou Wilt' on the rocky banks of the island. Local farmers saw this message and kindly brought him gifts of eggs, milk and corn!

Charles Jones also visited Crowley on Esopus Island. It is necessary here to note that Esopus Island was uninhabited before Crowley came. Jones had Crowley's magical diary for this time in his possession, but destroyed it 30 years later. This would seem to be just after Crowley's death. For some reason Jones had decided to resign from the OTO. Crowley blamed Jones wife for this, strangely. However when Crowley returned to New York in the September, Jones continued his Magical Alliance with Crowley, perhaps to perform sex magic. Their relationship resumed.

It was on Esopus Island that Crowley completed his translation of the Tao Te Ching, which was channelled through a 6th century Taoist Master. This Chinese guide and incarnation was named Ko Hsuen. Crowley's version is in prose and based on a version by the scholar James Legge.

FROM THE BOOK OF LIES:-

Chinese Music

"Explain this Happening!"
'It must have a Natural Cause' }
"It must have a Supernatural Cause" }
Let....These 2 asses must be set to grind corn.
May, Might, Must
Should, probably, Maybe,
We may safely assume,
Ought, it is hardly questionable,
Almost certainly,
Poor Hacks!
Let them be turned out to grass!
Proof is only possible in Mathematics!
And Mathematics is only a matter of arbitrary conventions.
And Yet doubt is a good servant, But a bad Master;
A perfect mistress, but a nagging wife
"White is White", is the lash of the overseer,
"White is Black", is the watchword of the slave
The Master takes no Heed
The Chinese cannot help thinking that
The Octave has 5 notes
The more necessary anything appears to my mind
The more certain it is that I only assert a limitation
I slept with Faith, and found a corpse in my arms on awakening,
I drank and danced all Night with Doubt, and found her a Virgin in the
morning".

This beautiful and magical poem or treatise explores would-be certainties and finds them wanting, wipes away platitudes and Blind Faith. Crowley asserts himself as a Magus and Master who 'does not concern himself with facts'. He does not care if a thing is true or not, he uses truth and falsehood indiscriminately to serves his ends'. He asserts therefore that all Truth is relative. Crowley lived by this creed. Indeed it is fundamental to "Do What Thou wilt shall be the Whole of the Law"

On the long and winding road that is his spiritual and magical journey Crowley deduced through his magical working with Jones and Neuberg amongst others that he had lived various past lives which led to his current one. At the time of Lao Tsu who composed the Tao Te Ching he, Crowley, was a disciple of this Master and named Ko Hsuen. Crowley completed his own writings on Tao Te Ching (The Way of the Tao) on Esopus Island. The Guide Amalantrah assisted him with this through magic and ritual. Charles Jones may well have been present during some of this discourse. He was later subject to the Doubt of the above poem.

New York Public Library

Crowley returned to New York and described to Seabrook the knowledge he had gained as they walked through Manhattan to Fifth Avenue and the New York Public Library. Jones came to stay with Crowley when he found an apartment at University Place, Washington Square towards the end of 1918. They again travelled to Detroit to meet with a group of Masons who lived there, though this proved fruitless. However Crowley composed enough material to create Vol. 3 of The Equinox which was published in March 1919.

Affluent Detroit March 1918

Within what has come to be known as the 'Blue Equinox', Crowley wrote encouragingly of Charles Jones as his magical colleague and spiritual son. Jones moved to Chicago for a while and then returned to his wife in Vancouver. He was becoming interested in the Kabbalah due to his own spiritual insights. Jones wrote a book 'Liber 31' which included this inner wisdom revealed to him. Crowley, upon reading it saw him as the Child of the New Aeon, and also an Ipsissimus of the A:.A:. Grade 10o - 1o possibly higher in grade than Crowley. Crowley was certainly shaken by what he read.

However Crowley had at this time a diversion, a new Scarlet Woman, Leah Hirsig, 35 years old and a teacher, from the Bronx. She had a son Hansi whom Crowley named Dyonisus; his father having disappeared from his life completely. Leah became Crowley's lover, magical consort and confidante, helping him to establish the Law of Thelema. Leah's sister, Alma Hirsig had firstly introduced Crowley to Leah. Alma was very interested in the Occult and worked for a Magician called Pierre Bernard. Later she would write a book about her experiences called "My Life in a Love Cult: A Warning to All Young Girls" by Marion Dockerill (her pseudonym)! Alma and Leah may well have indulged in sibling rivalry, with one being the High Priestess and the other the Scarlet Woman. They had come from a home of 9 children with an abusive and alcoholic father. Her mother had bravely taken all 9 children, 5 sisters and four brothers away from Switzerland to America .Alma and Leah called on Crowley at his studio where he had been painting. He was instantly attracted to Alma and kissed her. The sisters left and he did not meet Leah again until January 1919.

LEAH HIRSIG

Crowley telephoned Leah to come and model for him. She modelled nude and after the painting was finished they became lovers. He named her Alostrael - The Womb or Grail of God. She had the effect of inspiring him to action he said. In February 1919 they moved to 63 Washing Square South together. This was an altogether more opulent apartment with easy chairs, tapestries and fine rugs. That summer he planned another Great Magical Retirement to Montauk On Long Island.

Washington Square, New York

This Magical Retirement lasted a short time and was not very productive. Crowley decided to take a trip to Decatur, Atlanta to visit Seabrook and his wife Kate, who he knew from Greenwich Village.
Here he became involved in sex magic with Kate with Seabrook's consent. They were the greatest of friends he later said.

Ed Jackson

ATLANTA CITY HALL 1918

Late Summer 1918 was his last sojourn in America to Atlanta. He returned to New York, realising that his work in America was at an end and that he had achieved little. He later said that he was "too young, too ignorant and too biased to make an impression on the United States". In late December, after an asthma attack, he returned to London. He left behind him a string of worthless cheques said his friend Frank Harris. He had never visited Rhode Island.

CROWLEY'S HEALTH BEGINS TO DOMINATE HIS LIFE

On arrival in London Crowley went to see a Doctor in Harley Street in December 1919. This Doctor prescribed heroin for both asthma and severe bronchitis. Crowley had occasionally used heroin in the past but from this point on his use became an addiction. He was almost 45 years old. After staying briefly at his Aunts' house in Croydon, Crowley went to Paris. Leah Hirsig was waiting in France for him with little Hansi and was pregnant. Here, with Leah, he sought to bring the Word of Thelema to Europe and to scale new magical heights. It was 2nd January 1920. In Paris he met not only Leah but also Ninette Shumway, a widow she had made friends with on the ship over to France. Ninette had a small boy of 3 years old named Howard. She too decided to work for Crowley and became his second magical lover. Leah was still his Scarlet Woman and Ninette he named Sister Cypris, a magical helper.

Paris 1920

Crowley now had a ready made family of two women with two sons and a new baby on the way. He had obtained roughly £3000 in inheritances and decided to move to a rural setting at 11 bis Rue de Neuville in Fountainebleau. Where they remained until early March.

Pretty Fountainebleau Today

On 20th February, Leah gave birth to a daughter, Anne Leah also nicknamed Poupee. Crowley sent Leah to London for a few weeks, to obtain medical care for the baby. Ninette and Crowley looked for somewhere less expensive than Fountainbleau. He consulted the I Ching on 1st March about Cefalu in Italy and obtained an auspicious reading.

In a past life Crowley saw that he was Count Cagliostro, born Guiseppe Balsamo a Sicilian peasant. He rose, in the 18th Century to become a Master of Magic with links to free masonry. He died in Rome, a prisoner of the Inquisition. Cefalu was on his Path of Destiny. So by 1st April they had arrived in Cefalu a pretty fishing town with cobbled streets and a large Norman Cathedral. They leased a house called the Villa Santa Barbara on the South Eastern outskirts of Cefalu. Crowley would in time rename this Villa as the Abbey of Thelema. There was, once more, a family around him. Leah and Poupee arrived on 14th April. Crowley felt energised and ascended a Rock which overlooks Cefalu. Like the King of the Castle he surveyed his realm. At the Abbey of Thelema they would found the New Aeon. It is useful here to mention that Saint Barbara was a saint from the first century who rejected Paganism and converted to Christianity. She was murdered by her father. Before this she was imprisoned and tortured by the Romans. Even though she suffered greatly, many miracles were performed during her imprisonment and each morning her wounds had miraculously healed. Eventually the Romans had had enough of her and asked her father to execute her. After he did this he was struck by lightning and killed on his way home. In 1969 Pope Paul IV decided she was fictitious and struck her off as a Saint. (?)

The Abbey of Thelema Today

There is no doubt that the Abbey of Thelema was an Oasis, a Healing Space in Crowley's Life. Were the meanderings of his life journey to India, Burma, Canada and America merely distractions off his Life Path? Certainly a huge amount of money had been spent which, had he looked ahead, would have allowed the Abbey to exist for longer, either in Sicily or perhaps even France. Yet Crowley was not a planner he was 'of the moment'. He saw the bounty Life offered him as his Right, and the times of famine as the work of enemies, of others, nothing to do with him. Perhaps the Tao Te Ching had some words of Wisdom in this regard.

"35. The Good Will of the Teh. The whole World is drawn to him that hath the likeness of the Tao. Men flock unto him, and suffer no ill, but gain repose, find peace, enjoy all ease.
Sweet sounds and cakes lure the traveler from his way. But the Word of the Tao, though it appears harsh and insipid, unworthy to hearken to or to behold, hath his use all inexhaustible". So this was a time of no worries as only good could come of this venture.

China 1906

CROWLEY IN ITALIAN PEASANT GUISE WITH NINETTE SHUMWAY AND HANSI, HOWARD AND BABY ANNE LEAH

As a painter Crowley was inspired by the Artist Paul Gauguin who lived in Tahiti. Gauguin, Crowley felt, had understood the values and beliefs of Thelema and he included him in the Gnostic Mass. Following his desire to continue painting Crowley painted murals on the walls of the Villa and particularly in the Inner Temple.

The Villa could see Palermo to the West, and the Sea to the East. Behind it to the North was the large rock Cephaloedium, further in front of the Villa and to the South, trees and an Olive Grove. The walk from Cefalu was up a long and winding mountain path. The Abbey was primitive. There was no bathroom or proper kitchen with sink. Five rooms lead off from a central hall or 'Sanctum Sanctorum'. this room had an alter with six candles. Crowley had his own bedroom and had painted murals on the walls of the other rooms.

Temple of Diana, Cefalu, Italy

There can be no doubt that this Villa was auspiciously placed in the town. It had views of the Rock behind them and the Temples there, and also of the houses below and even out to sea. There were high hopes for the Magical achievements here.

Jane Wolfe came to attend the Abbey as a student in 1920. She arrived from Bou Saada in July 1920, feeling positive and full of life, enchanted by Cefalu. She wrote of the 2 little boys, "They were dear little fellows of 4 and 6 at this time. And how they did adore being with their Mothers. But this did not satisfy AC. The boys had to break the Gordian knot. So sandwiches were packed and the boys were ordered to take a walk somewhere. Hansi behind trees did not last long. Our little boys took themselves hither and thither, exploring the countryside. Hansi frequently returning with a trailing robe or none at all. Howie was always clothed. But Hansi was a little animal of the woods. The peasants adored him and gave him their superb bread. I would be glad if such bread like that came my way today. Hansi had manna from heaven at all times. But Leah was busy with Crowley's work. I taught the boys poetry, the stars and the planets".

By January 1922 she wrote "I composed myself with 2 doses of heroin as my mind was hopping about. Did not know what God I wished to invoke? After a time my whole being radiated Love towards one who seemed to be in my room........I felt on a brink and could not plunge now.........."
Dec 22 "In the afternoon the Beast came in to wish me a Happy New Year. The sorrow rose again. I felt like weeping up my boot heels and went out for a solitary walk. But it availed me naught. Physically too tired to go far..."
Wolfe came in like a Lion and went out like a lamb. She was undermined and destroyed by heroin and her self esteem plummeted. However the early days at the Abbey were heady and allowed for a communion with Nature. Crowley was elated with two women and his ready made family. He called his bedroom the Room of Nightmares. Certainly his rituals and magic were attracting many energies to The Abbey of Thelema. I have calculated this Villa to, at the back, be in the North, Crowley's area for Disaster in the Pa Kua No7, and the front to be facing South, South East, and East. These areas correspond to South, the 5 Ghosts, South East, Unlucky Influences and East, Death.

East is not a good area for a bedroom and would be better as a storeroom. South, the area of 5 Ghosts is an area where any magical or ritual work will conjure up spirits of those long departed who once dwelt in the building. A good room for mediumship but not for rituals such as those of Jane Wolfe who felt haunted during her work and very lonely.
South East, an area of accidents or physical injury. Not good as a kitchen, childrens room, bathroom, the area for Death potentially.

Crowley sought to encourage new students to his Abbey by writing a brochure. He told students what to expect from their Study at the Abbey. His painting and murals contained lurid descriptions and figures which he assured would "pass students of the Sacred Wisdom through the ordeal of contemplating every possible phantom which can assail the soul". The secret process of this would include one or more drugs, opium, ether,cocaine, heroin, laudanum, hashish and anhalonium. Leah Hirsig was his Scarlet Woman and He the Great Beast; he swore an oath of allegiance to her.
Rituals and magic now took on a new depth and defilement. As he endured more so he expected others to do so too.

Interestingly, he seems to have found time for recreation in Palermo nearby where he met male prostitutes for sex. At the same time both Leah Hirsig and Ninette Shumway became pregnant by Crowley in 1920. Anne (Poupee) still remained in poor health. Crowley wailed about this but seemed impotent to intervene. Nothing was done and Anne, (Poupee) died in hospital on 14 October 1920. Jane Wolfe was by now staying with Crowley and must surely have been a help. Hirsig was devastated and six days later miscarried. The loss of two babies at this time must have caused the onset of post-natal depression which can make a woman prone to all manner of illusions. Leah became convinced that Ninette was working black magic against her. Ninette Shumway was banished to Cefalu town and gave birth to her daughter there on 5th November 1920.
Crowley's ideal family was starting to unravel and he was demented with the reality of it. He wrote, "I am utterly appalled at the horrors of the human heart. I never dreamed such things were possible. I am physically sick. It is the greatest shock of my Life. I had this mess in my own Circle. I poisoned my work. I murdered my children".

The Abbey continued as a place for students though and charged 50 guineas for 3 months. Crowley yearned to train new souls in Thelema in an evangelistic fashion.
In the temple the Men wore blue robes, with hoods lined in red; the Women wore blue robes with hoods lined in gold. The Thelemites would bathe in the nude in the sea and were asked to climb the Rock behind the Abbey in ritual and meditation.

Abbey of Thelema in the 1950s

Cecil Frederick Russell, an American arrived at the Abbey on 21st November 1920. He had met Crowley before in America after reading 'The Revival of Magick' in the International. This time he came to study 'The Book of the Law'. Crowley wanted Russell to explore the kabbalistic mysteries. He was attracted to Russell yet nervous of his brashness and realised that Russell was unaccepting of Crowley's authority. Russell by turn resisted Crowley's attempts to seduce him through sexual magic, over the coming months. Crowley, for his part was disgusted with himself at how much he desired Russell. Russell left the Abbey of Thelema in Autumn 1921. Crowley had not seduced him and his magical teachings were also an anticlimax. Russell wrote of his experience, "Crowley was first, last and always an author.....and this was always on his mind; so is it any wonder that Magick sometimes did not achieve his anticipated results! Ever hunting the happy phrase, modelling the merriest metaphor - even while fucking he was recording the Opus in his mind rather than endeavouring to establish focussed energy to effect Samadhi! Like a professional Magician deceiving Destiny with misdirection not realising Fate was his own Higher Self". How True!

Cecil Frederick Russell - the Mathematician

Crowley went to Paris in Spring 1921 to drum up new students for the Abbey. He met up with John William Navin Sullivan and his wife Sylvia. Crowley and Sylvia became lovers. Truth to tell he was bored of the Abbey and wanted a change of scene. Initially Sullivan was not jealous of Crowley's affair with his wife but that situation changed. They did not come with him to Cefalu. He returned to the Abbey subdued and continued his painting of murals. He was also using Heroin in greater quantities. The more he took the more he desired to be free of its enslavement now.
New visitors came in the Spring and Summer of 1921. One was Captain M E Townsend, a friend of J F C Fuller. Townsend was serving in the War Office and Crowley hope to impress him and thus impress Fuller. He wrote a letter to Fuller saying "Your friendship stands out as the best thing in my life of that kind……I know it was mostly the fault of my silly pride (that we fell out)…"
But Fuller did not reply.

At the end of June 1921 Mary Butts a writer and her lover Cecil Maitland arrived to spend 3 months at the Abbey and receive instruction in Magick.
Mary and Cecil were a romantic couple who had met Crowley in Paris. Maitland was the son of an Anglican Clergyman who had converted to Catholicism, which fascinated Crowley. They both joined in the rituals and magical ceremonies as much as they could though Mary felt she had to refuse a ceremonial cake Crowley offered her which she said was a goat's turd.

Mary Butts

Mary and Cecil returned to London in September 1921. They both felt their time at the Abbey had injured their health and they both had become addicted to heroin. Mary Butts died of peritonitis in 1937 from an operation on a perforated ulcer. During her stay with Crowley she had helped editorially with 'Magick in Theory and Practice'
The Thelemic Message had a more positive effect on Frank Bennett who also

arrived in the Summer of 1921 and stayed for 4 months. Frank was 53, and an Australian Bricklayer. He had lived in London in 1909 and read the Equinox, then joined the OTO. He left Cefalu an Adeptus Major in the A:.A:.
Bennett was released from sexual inhibitions at the Abbey, which created within him a sense of well being. He went back to Australia in late 1921.

Frank Bennett

THE ABBEY OF THELEMA AS A TEMPLE AND A HOME

In Feng Shui we would be trying to encourage beneficial chi into the building. The inner room used as a temple would be prone to stagnant energy or sha chi. Beneficial Chi would be introduced through a pond or fountain outside the home, and airing the building frequently. Since sliding into addiction Crowley and his family and visitors did nothing about the dirt and decay which grew. Dust, dirt and decay in Feng Shui create Sha chi; negative energy which produces lack of growth, lack of energy, stagnation and lack of creativity. Crowley's Natal number was 7 and the Trigram Tui, West. There was a need to move home to a more favourable environment. His natal number was 9, South, Yang, Fire and East. To ease this contradiction a move to North Africa would have benefited them all. Cleaning the Abbey on a regular basis would have cleared much of the Sha Chi. Encouraging beneficial Chi into a home is vital and Chi has a need to flow and meander. It should not be expected to leave by the same entrance it came in. Dead areas are where the current of Chi is unable to flow. Mirrors are helpful to encourage positive Chi, also crystals, though they are not useful in bedrooms as they disturb the body in repose and can give disturbing dreams. It would also seem that the flow of water to the site was not monitored. Whether there was a well, or water had to be fetched, and Jane Wolfe's diaries indicate that there was - it would seem that the flow of water was not close to the site, and in an unfavourable direction.

Ill Health was frequent in most of those who stayed at the Abbey of Thelema. When the Winter of 1922 came Crowley travelled once more to Paris. It was February and Leah Hirsig had come with him. Again they stayed at 50 Rue Vavin off the Boulevard Montparnasse. Leah went on to London, probably to see a Doctor. Crowley was adrift, alone in Paris. The old excitement and creativity no longer interested him. He was near to collapse due to his heroin and cocaine addictions. As with so many addicts before him, and many since he thought that he could master his addiction alone. On 14 February he went to Fountainebleau to stay at an auberge, 'Au Cadran Blue'. Here he struggled to reduce the intake of the drugs. Crowley, even in his 'Book of the Law' had never managed moderation, it was not in his nature. Now it was essential to his well being and he realised it. Leah had joined him and the 2 of them travelled to London in May 1922.

Charming Fountainebleau today

From Fountainebleau they found a flat in Russell Square, London. Crowley renewed old acquaintances and sold some old belongings. He must have been concerned at Leah's illness also.

Russell Square Today

In reality Crowley had abandoned the Abbey of Thelema during this Summer of May 1922, for London and for sources of income. He went to Wellington Square, Chelsea to visit Gerald Kelly. Kelly had taken on responsibility for Lola Zaza who was now 14 years old. She was there for Crowley's visit and had not seen him since 1910. She had become a petulant teenager! Crowley wrote, "Lola Zaza is unmanageable. She despises everybody, thinks she is a genius , yet is stupid, inaccurate, plain, ill-tempered etc. God its good to be a Lion (leo). For the first time in my Life I taste the true pleasures of immortality......."
Lola Zaza never again saw her father. She became a nursery governess, and later married. Sadly she disowned her father completely.

On 13th May 1922 Crowley went to the War Office to see Fuller. In fact Fuller refused to see him and sent him a cutting note saying 'Nothing Doing'. However Crowley continued to write to him from time to time for some years hence.
He next went to visit Austin Harrison of 'The English Review'. This was a beneficial visit and Harrison took on Crowley as a contributor to The English Review over the Summer. Remuneration was not huge but there was creative freedom for Crowley. He wrote 'The Great Drug Delusion' and also 'The Drug Panic' for the June and July issues 1922. Crowley also spoke to a Grant Richards and offered to write a book on 'the drug traffic insanity'. He called it 'The Diary of a Drug Fiend' and was offered a £60 advance if he delivered the manuscript within a month. So Crowley took lodgings with Leah Hirsig at 31 Wellington Street, Chelsea. They worked together on the manuscript in a fury. 'The Diary of a Drug Fiend' was initially published by Collins who were so pleased with it that they advanced him £120 for a second book - a full autobiography. This time he took 7 years to complete the manuscript and it was called 'Confessions'. The Sunday Express, who had castigated James Joyce ,'Ulysses' earlier that year, roundly thrashed Crowley's work, 'The Diary of a Drug Fiend'. It further slated him by writing of
'Orgies in Sicily'. In fact 'Diary of a Drug Fiend' was a book of its times and a work of popular fiction. It was also a very idealised account of life at the Abbey of Thelema, and a book of romantic fiction addressed to a female popular audience. A Mills and Boon of its day!

Crowley and Leah returned to Cefalu in October 1922. Jane Wolfe wrote of this in her Diary on 4th October , "Leah has changed considerably. She is noticeably freer of the personal. I assume this is a permanent change, though her illness (Dr. Maggio says 'Tuberculosis' and shakes his head) may explain a part of it. She lacks her former 'pep'. I have now finished two coats, one for Howie and one for Hansi, made out of two coats of the Beast, dug out of a trunk". She also wrote, "To see her no one would suspect an illness of nervous breakdown".

Jane Wolfe

Before leaving Cefalu in 1923, Jane wrote of her experiences, ".... After retiring I realised that in order to fully complete herself Woman had to achieve something in which Man had no part. Ie, Woman may give up her entire life to helping Man achieve his Will; it is not sufficient for her. I have a message for Woman - 'You thought of my Tea' ie Woman's Affairs; Now did it out Mine the Cup and the Disk, Beast the Wand and the Sword, thus completing the Whole".

If Crowley thought that a book on taking drugs was going to attract new students to the Abbey at Cefalu he was deluded. Collins the publisher was urged to withdraw the novel 'Diary of a Drug Fiend' by the Sunday Express. To their credit they did not but once the edition was sold out they did not reprint. It remains a time capsule of upper class depravity and drug taking during the 1920s by Sir Peter Pendragon and his wife, Unlimited Lou. Rescued by a Wise Lord they are saved by the Abbey of Thelema and its philosophy.

Frederick Charles Loveday Known as Raoul

Raoul Loveday came to Cefalu with his new wife Betty May in November 1922. Crowley had met them in London that same May. Though lower middle class Loveday had won a scholarship to Oxford and graduated with a First in History from St John's College. He was very interested in Egyptology and the Occult. He was an attractive man with fairish hair high cheekbones and deep eyes. Betty May was an artists model and several years older than Raoul. She had been married twice before. Betty had sat for the sculptor Jacob Epstein for his bust 'The Savage'. She had also briefly met Crowley before. It was Betty Bickers a mutual acquaintance who had introduced Raoul to Crowley. Betty May had this to say when Raoul returned from his meeting with the Great Beast, "...when he came home he was covered in soot and dust and his breath reeked of ether. I put him to bed and he lay in a doped sleep until the middle of the following day. When he awoke I found out that he had spent the whole time he had been away with the great mystic and that he had taken the drug to excite the mystical activities of his soul".

Betty May had previously been a Cocaine Addict, but now took a dim view of Loveday's interest with drugs and Crowley. She sought to get her husband to give up both.

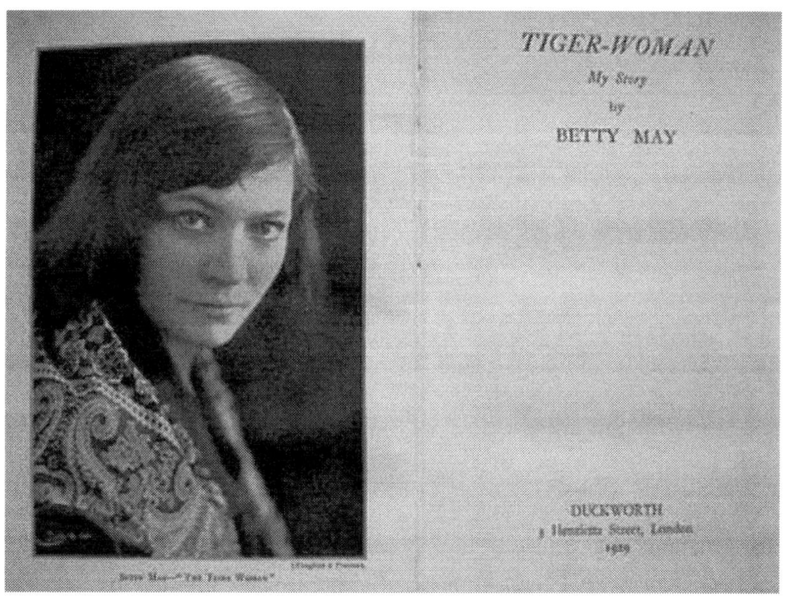

Betty May and her Autobiography

It is clear that Betty was madly in love with Raoul. She had come to Cefalu in their honeymoon period and also to support Raoul who she saw as entering the Lion's den. Crowley saw Loveday as the student he had been searching for, and perhaps a successor to Victor Neuberg. That Crowley must have been attracted to Raoul is undeniable.. When they arrived at the Abbey, Crowley gave his usual greeting, 'Love is the Law, Love under Will'. Betty May's frosty response was 'Good Evening'. Crowley, annoyed, demanded that she follow form and so this was the first of a number of harsh exchanges between them both. The honeymoon couple were at odds in the Abbey. Raoul wanted to follow the teachings and guidance of his Master. Betty May was forced to fit in with an odd communal household. It was late December before they had their own separate room. They had to cut themselves with razors if they used the word 'I'. Betty of course would have none of it. Raoul took this seriously but could not help saying 'I' and so was covered in cuts! In January 1923 Raoul became ill. Betty initially thought it was drug use or the toxic effect of consuming cat's blood. Loveday had been asked to sacrifice a cat by Crowley. He slashed its neck and drank its blood. However the local doctor Dr. Maggio came and diagnosed an infection caused by drinking water from the local mountain spring. Crowley had in fact warned the couple about drinking from local springs, when they had gone off on a hiking expedition. However Raoul's illness was much worse in the February, and he told Betty he had been suffering from diarrhea and fever for 10 days. He felt very weak and said he wanted to return to England.

Betty wrote to Raoul's mother that Raoul was too weak to be moved and that Crowley was a tyrant to them, " He is laying down all sorts of rules, that could not possibly be kept. I have never worked so hard in my life as I am here. I am very ill myself, but I am looking after Raoul as best I can. He wants a good warm bed and nourishment which he cannot get here. If Raoul gets better Crowley thinks of parting us and what can we do. We have got no money and are dependent upon him for our food". Crowley and Hirsig have different versions of this. However Crowley was annoyed at Betty for reading which was expressly forbidden, even English newspapers sent by Raoul's mother, fortnightly at Raoul's request were forbidden.

The confrontational argument between Crowley and Betty came on 11th February 1923. She informs us in her diary " I had not been reading long when the Mystic strode in, his face twitching with rage. He ordered me to go. There was a terrific scene. I should have said before that there were several loaded revolvers which used to lie about the Abbey. They were very necessary for we never knew whether brigands might not attack it. The Mystic used to shoot any dogs that came anywhere near the Abbey with his revolver. He was an extremely good shot. It so happened that I found one of these revolvers lying about the day before, and it suddenly occurred to me that it would be a wise precaution to hide it under my pillow. I now seized it and fired it wildly at the Mystic. It went wide of the mark. He laughed heartily. Then I rushed at him but could not get a grip on his shaved head. He picked me up in his arms and flung me bodily outside, through the front door!"

Their room was a wrecked. Raoul was moved to Crowley's room and Betty went down into Cefalu. Crowley became worried about the sympathy Betty might receive from both British and Sicilian authorites. The next day he sent Jane Wolfe down to visit Betty and learn her intentions. May told her that she had sent a telegram to Raoul's father and asked him to contact the Consul in Palermo and the Commissario in Cefalu. Wolfe returned to the Abbey and wrote a letter dictated by Loveday which asked Betty to return. Betty did so and was asked to sign an affidavit drawn up by Hirsig as a condition of re-entry.

However Raoul Loveday's illness worsened and on St Valentine's day Dr Maggio was summoned and diagnosed acute entiritis. Crowley wrote in his Diary, "I feel a current of Magical force - heavy, black and silent - threatening the Abbey". It did not occur to him that he might have summoned it. He cast the horoscope for Raoul Lovelday and predicted, "A gloomy depression. Its looks as though you might die on 16th February at 4 o'clock" This did indeed come to pass for poor Raoul Loveday.

Crowley noted in his Diary, "Raoul developed paralysis of the heart and died at once without fear or pain. It was as if a man, tired of staying indoors, had gone out for a walk". Yet neither Crowley nor Betty May were there at his parting; and perhaps this is what he wished.

After 3 days money arrived for Betty May from the British Consulate. Leah had drafted a letter to them which Betty signed. Crowley and Betty remained calm with one another. After the funeral Crowley became ill and bedridden with bouts of fever for several weeks. Leah and Jane Wolfe nursed him. Jane Wolfe

was sent to London to try to raise some funds for the Abbey at the end of February.
Betty May was interviewed by the Sunday Express who by now had a vendetta going against Crowley. They ran an article on 25th February 1923 headlined "New Sinister Relations of Aleister Crowley. Varsity Lad's Death. Dreadful Ordeal of a Young Wife". It was both lurid and melodramatic. However it was the final nail in the coffin to any designs Crowley had on a career as a writer and poet and established Spiritual Master. He was pilloried in some parts of the press Those without integrity who had come into contact with him made hay in the media. William Seabrook in America for example catered to the Heart Sunday tabloid chain. His reputation had been damaged beyond repair. He had no way of countering this and his arrogance and foolishness did not even seek any damage limitation.

On April 22nd 1923 Crowley was waiting for yet another student to arrive. He was a colleague of Victor Neuberg's and his name was Norman Mudd. This was unfortunate as an Order Of Expulsion was served to Crowley the next day in the Office of the Commissario of Cefalu. Crowley asked for a week to prepare for his departure. This was granted and Norman Mudd and Ninette Shumway were to stay behind and take care of the Abbey. Leah Hirsig would leave with Crowley. Mussolini was in power at this time in Italy and the negative publicity may have reflected badly on the regime of the fascists.

The Abbey of Thelema was an unmitigated disaster and the death toll was high. Few could have tolerated the insanitary conditions and lack of basic amenities, even for the 1920s. The drug taking was an indulgence which Crowley had not needed when he first began his magical operations or even the Abra-melin.
He had slumped into addiction when his high ideals in Magic and Literature were not achieved. He clutched at straws with the arrival of each new student. Eventually they became merely monetary gain to fuel his exiled existence from London and the society he hoped to impress. It was time to go home.

CROWLEY - THE WILD ROVER

From The Tao Te Ching by Lao Tzu by Aleister Crowley; No 39
The Law of the Beginning;
"These things have possessed the Tao from the beginning; Heaven, clear and shining; Earth, steady and easy; Spirits, mighty in Magic; Vehicles, overflowing with Joy; all that hath Life; and the rulers of men. All these derive their essence from the Tao.
Without the Tao, Heaven would dissolve, Earth disrupt, Spirits become impotent; Vehicles empty; living things would perish and rulers lose their power.
The root of grandeur is Humility; and the strength of exaltation in its base. Thus rulers speak of themselves as 'Fatherless', 'Virtueless', 'Unworthy', proclaiming by this that their Glory is in their shame. So also the virtue of a Chariot is not any of the parts of a Chariot, if they be numbered. They do not seek to appear fine like Jade, but inconspicuous, like common stone".
So modesty and humility must now be the order of the day. Crowley consulted the I Ching for new locations. Somehow, it told him to go to Tunisia which was under French rule. On 1st May 1923 they sailed from Palermo to the Port of Tunis, Crowley and Leah Hirsig together. By 11th May they had found a cheap room in an hotel 'Au Souffle du Zephir' in La Marsa Plage, a tourist town, North East of Tunis.

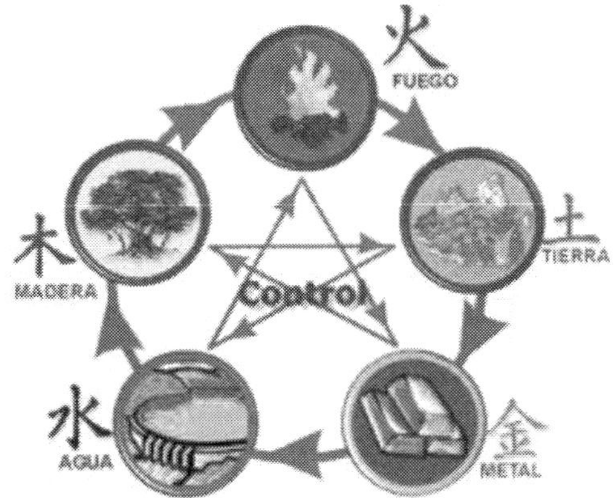

La Marsa, Plage

Crowley was now ill with drug dependence. He was still trying to wean himself off heroin using cocaine, luminal or ethyl oxide. He suffered from insomnia, dyspnoea, diarrhea and days lost in thought or dreaming. Even so he struggled on, dictating to Leah the book 'Confessions'. Ninette Shumway was looking after the children at the Abbey and Leah returned to see them over the summer.
Ninette had been pregnant and gave birth to a daughter on 19th May 1923. The father was Baron La Calce, the Landlord of the Abbey but he took no responsibility for his daughter. Crowley named Ninette's daughter, Isabella, Isis, Selene, Hecate, Artemis, Diana, Hera, Jane. Ninette stayed on at the Abbey until 1924 when the dastardly Baron evicted her for non-payment of rent. Ninette also had another daughter by Crowley named Astarte, Lulu, Panthea, as well as her son Howard. She also looked after Hansi, Leah's son.

Crowley had reached his lowest ebb in many ways. He had no publisher for his book and he had lost the Abbey of Thelema. He at last became introspective and analysed his actions, even at one point writing in his Diary "Why drag out a useless life, dishonouring my reputation, discrediting my methods etc?" he even considered Suicide. Crowley looked back over his past, his childhood and his christian upbringing. At the end of the day he deduced that "I may be a Black Magician but I'm a bloody great one!...." This perked him up and he realised that the work had to be continued and that students such as Norman Mudd, devoted, inquisitive, esoteric, had to be taught.

Leah Hirsig and Jane Wolfe at Cefalu

Norman Mudd had supported Crowley at Cambridge in 1910 but was not a central figure because at that time Crowley was enamoured of Victor Neuberg. Mudd later went to South Africa and became Head of Department in Applied Mathematics at Grey University College, Bloemfontain. He lost the sight in one eye due to gonorrhea and was single for many years. However he came to London to seek out Crowley in 1920. Crowley was by then in Cefalu but Mudd thought he was in America and thus went to Detroit. There he met Charles Robert Stansfeld Jones or Frater Achad. Norman Mudd became a student of Jones. Eventually he made contact with Crowley, who asked for some financial recompense and invited Mudd to Cefalu. Mudd returned to South Africa on 12 April 1921.

Charles Robert Stansfeld Jones or Frater Achad

Once there he read the letters Crowley had sent him in 1921 which he had been unable to answer. He decided to leave his position as teacher, sell his possessions and set sail for Cefalu. Thus he arrived on 22nd April 1923 and undertook an administrative and caretaking role for Crowley at the Abbey. Crowley wrote to Mudd that his career since 1904 "...for these 19 years has been a brilliant failure...." but he felt he could trust Mudd. Crowley was a broken man at this point in his Life and Mudd may well have recognised this. His loyalty and hard work was commendable. He wrote to the Oxford University Magazine 'Isis' on 14 November 1923, praising Crowley. He also wrote a pamphlet "An Open Letter To Lord Beaverbrook" which he had printed and sent to British literary and political figures. He cited the lies about Crowley in the Sunday Express and explained how Crowley could not bear litigation costs. He championed Crowley and he demanded fair play.

Crowley, weak and insecure left Leah at La Marsa and took a room at the Tunisia Palace Hotel with a young black male Mohammed ben Brahim with whom he had a sexual relationship. He said he had hired him as a servant to perform sex magic with. However, though unwell, he desired this man.

The mystical and romantic country of Tunisia, once a highlight of magical operations had become a backwater for him. It was also a place where Crowley could easily find heroin or opium and his will to fight his addiction diminished. Furthermore Norman Mudd had fallen in love with Leah Hirsig. Having worked closely with her Mudd desired her and asked Crowley if he might marry her. Crowley still felt an ownership of Leah and would not hear of such a thing, even though Leah felt affection for Norman Mudd. In his diary Norman wrote of Crowley's 'attitude of possession'. It certainly seems like a very old fashioned thing to have to do for Mudd to have to ask Crowley's permission for them to marry. Hardly Thelemic! Crowley still wanted control over his Scarlet Woman and needed her at this stage. He sent Mudd to a nearby village in Tunisia for a Magical Retirement from 28th September to 8th October.

Crowley continued living in Tunisia at Nefta and although creative, writing poetry, was ill and bedridden, as was Leah. With Feng Shui we would have to look at the geographical locations to determine how Sha (negative Chi) is affecting these 2 people. Feng Shui would dictate that they have brought with them from Cefalu, Sha, negative energy. Sha, can come from geographical faults, Gulleys, Tunnels, corners of buildings, central passageways in a building, 'through' rooms and telegraph poles. Yet it is more likely that the Illness from Sha is the residue of what has happened in Sicily, and the lack of sanitary provision as well as the continuous drug taking and grief over 2 deaths. Recovery was an extremely slow process.

Tunis, Place de la Victoire

There is no doubt that the sun, light and dry atmosphere of North Africa was of benefit to Crowley and his asthma. It was at Au Cadran Bleu that he had tried to wean himself off of heroin and cocaine. Sadly he thought that the addiction was purely mental - and did not realise that it was both mental and physical. A Dr Edmund Gros in France had suggested that he attend a sanatorium in Divonne-Les-Bains, Aix. Crowley, after being prescribed luminal felt much better and decided against it. Leah at this time was suffering from the effects of drug poisoning, had night sweats and still had tuberculosis. Crowley was also very angry about the Sunday Express article and wrote to Frank Harris, "....Yesterday I decided to go to England the moment cash comes from Mudd and attack the Sunday Express with my naked hands..... I have tried in particular to combine my mission with living the life of an English Gentleman and the God's won't allow it.. They have check-mated my plans with ever increasing severity...." Yet whilst Crowley fought his addiction or socialised in the cafes of Paris, Norman Mudd was spending the night at the Metropolitan Asylums Board for the Homeless Poor in London. He gave his place of birth as Manchester.

TIME TO RETURN, TIME TO VISIT PARIS

Frank Harris, a friend of Crowley's and someone with whom he corresponded gave him the money to leave Tunisia by boat for France. He left Leah Hirsig behind and travelled to the Hotel de Blois at 50 Rue Vavin in Montparnasse, in late December 1923.

Montparnasse in 1925

Monsieur Bourcier who owned the Hotel de Blois was still owed money by Crowley but kindness and credit on his part still allowed him to entertain Crowley as a paying guest. Norman Mudd went to London to join Jane Wolfe who was at this time working at a Nursing Home there. Crowley visited Fountainebleau in February 1924, and was still using heroin for his asthma attacks. It was at this time that he decided to visit the Institute for the Harmonious Development of Man. Perhaps to see how Gurdjieff had been successful in running his own mystical organisation. This Institute had been set up by G I Gurdjieff, also a Mystic and Inspirational Speaker, who sought students. It was on 10th February that he visited the Chateau Prieure des Basses Loges

He was shown around by a Major Pindar as Gurdjieff was not there. Another historian James Webb tells a different story and said that Gurdieff was there, and that Crowley listened to Gurdjieff's music. When Crowley left on the Sunday evening and was at the door, Gurdjieff exploded at him, "You dirty, you filthy inside! Never again you set foot in my house..." This may or may not have occurred yet Crowley held no animosity towards Gurdjieff.

Leah Hirsig joined Crowley in Paris in March 1924. Crowley's health had broken down again and she looked after him. He even underwent surgery. They had no money though and he was evicted by Bourcier at the end of March. A Dr Jarvis recommended a Nursing home. Leah and Crowley that May stayed at the Au Cadrau Bleu Inn at Chelles Sur Marne. There would still be the small annuity from his mother and perhaps some royalties from writing that kept him going but his wealth and security in Life were now gone. It was time also to return to London. Still Crowley hung on to his wandering despite illness and poverty till the bitter end.

Chelles-Sur-Marne

Crowley now needed to travel in a favourable direction and that was West. He had lived too many times in places that were too Yin, including Chelles-Sur-Marne, a small town by the river and not even in the vibrant and energising centre of Paris. In fact it was east of Paris and a backwater. If ever there was a time to go back to England this was it. But Leah Hirsig was a follower, not a leader and did not initiate this. Thus they were both stuck in a rut. Leah knew she had come to the end of the line with Crowley when she wrote in her diary, "his rasping voice so jarred me that I wanted to scream". The end would come soon enough.

Figure 31.

THE KEY OF SOLOMON

SAVED - BY A NEW SCARLET WOMAN

Crowley was out of Luck, out of ideas, in ill health and in a backwater. In late August, by chance, he met Dorothy Olsen in Paris and within weeks they had become lovers, and she his next Scarlet Woman. Crowley callously dumped Leah Hirsig with whom he had grown tired and uninspired. It is important to remember also that she had seen him at his absolute worst. Yet she clung to him for three more years hoping against hope to once more regain her Scarlet Woman crown.

Dorothy Olsen was of Norwegian blood and from Wisconsin USA. She was thirty three, blond, warm, enthusiastic and direct. She was interested in Magic but not devoted to Crowley as Leah had been. When he brought Dorothy Olsen to his hotel room, Leah collapsed knowing that her position in his Life was over. Thus the next day, on 23 September 1924, Crowley and Olsen left for Marseilles, and from there to North Africa. Dorothy he gave the new name of Soror Astrid and initiated her into the A:.A:. They took a train to Tunis and thence to Sidi Bou Said in Tunisia.

Sidi Bou Said

Whilst travelling to Tunisia Crowley was guided by spirit guides or Secret Chiefs as he knew them to write a 'proclamation'. It was called "To Man", and proclaimed Crowley as the World teacher of the New Aeon. He directed his writing to the Theosophical Society under the leadership of Annie Besant and Charles W Leadbetter. They were nurturing their own World Teacher, Jiddu Krishnamurti, who of course, Crowley did not support. In fact Krishnamurti renounced this role anyway and still became one of the most widely read writers on Mysticism of the 20th century. A lesson in Humility. A lesson of the Tao.

Krishnamurti and Annie Besant

Crowley and Dorothy spent the Autumn of 1924 wandering along the Coast of Tunisia. He had his Magus ring made into a Jewel for Dorothy by a Tunisian jeweller. Leah was still in Paris. She had a telegram from Ninette Shumway to say that her sister Alma had come to Cefalu, and had taken Hansi, her son, back to America. Leah must surely have realised that the Abbey of Thelema was no more, for her or for Crowley. She wrote a depressing entry in her diary at this time and mourned for Anna Leah, little Poupee, her baby, remembering how she had passed away. She was cold and homeless having been evicted from the hotel on 28th September. Mudd left London on 30th September as she must have contacted him. They discussed the writing up of the 'Confessions' and their roles towards one another, she still seeing herself as the Scarlet Woman and he as her 'Son'.

Crowley did not return and so Mudd went back to London in December 1924. He would have asked Leah to accompany him. However she was still hanging on for Crowley. She found a job waitressing in Montparnasse in Winter 1924 in order to keep body and soul alive.

However, Leah's fortunes changed in late January 1925. Crowley contacted her and asked her to come to Tunis. Olsen was pregnant and Leah's help was needed. Leah went, and resumed her role as Secretary and helper to Crowley. She became pregnant by William George Barron whom Crowley knew, in Tunis. Dorothy Olsen was trying hard to have magical visions, in her role as Crowley's new Scarlet Woman, yet she had no magical vocation and was not gifted in this way. During this time also Crowley dealt a cruel blow to Dorothy which shattered the bone around her eye and left her needing medical care. She wrote to Norman Mudd in March 1925, ".....I am still alive in Tunis with many of the bones of my head removed. This is a good thing, It gives more room for my brain, such as it is, to expand...." Dorothy drank heavily and attacked Crowley just as Rose Kelly may have done. Crowley was at rock bottom and wanted an end to his difficulties and to his financial problems. Dorothy Olsen had not proved to be the answer to these.

WHERE AM I NOW? - THE LAW OF PERPETUAL MOTION

I've always felt that Aleister Crowley seemed confused and uncertain in the above picture. Certainly this was a time when radical change was needed in his life and instead he clung to the same old patterns. He had met a woman who he had used and abused and been unable to completely give up his heroin use. This had happened several times now in his Life.
In Feng Shui we would say that this is the Law of Perpetual Motion. If you repeat an action a sufficient number of times it becomes self-perpetuating. Feng Shui is the Art of working out and influencing someone's destiny. Feng Shui can be applied to your home, your career, your travels, virtually anything. Everything in the Universe works in cycles of expansion and contraction, whether it is climatic changes or the lifespan of a person or a career.

There is an expression in China that says that there are 3 things which can forecast the future. First there is Destiny. Next there is Feng Shui. Thirdly there is Luck. Destiny is mapped out for you; you were born with a certain Nature and react to events in a predictable fashion. Feng Shui makes the most of what you already have. It makes sure you are facing in the right direction; and doing the right thing at the right time. Luck - is when you are facing the right direction and in the right place at the right time anyway.

To Daoists and the Tao, Life is in a constant state of flux. Nothing is fixed The Tao has a moderating influence over everything and operates in a way that the Tao Te Ching describes as fanning. Thus, if anything is pushed too far, it will be restored by the Tao to its previous condition. This effect is like the swing of a pendulum. Lao Tsu asks his students to hold fast to the submissive. This means leading a simple life - free from desires and ambitions that inevitably cause a reversal of fortune. In troubled political times, holding fast to the submissive may also enable a person to avoid an untimely Death. Crowley realised much of what the Tao Te Ching was saying later in his life. What he sought was a Reversal of Fortune.

Leah Hirsig arrived to assist Crowley at the end of March 1925. Unfortunately Dorothy Olsen miscarried. She and Crowley left for France at the beginning of May. Leah was relieved and had begun to detach from Crowley. She had also made 2 friends Gerard Aumont who translated 'Diary of a Drug Fiend' into French and also William George Barron, whom she had met in Paris and with whom she performed sexual rituals. Leah recognised that her love for Crowley was an illness of the mind and she must get cured of it. She called it 'AC-itis'. She saw now that she was letting go of him.

Norman Mudd also saw that Aleister Crowley the Guru he followed and Aleister Crowley the person were quite different. He had idealised him. He wrote, "AC is a coward and a shirker. He puts his dirty work on to others". Victor Neuberg had found this out also, to his cost. However being the loyal person that he was Norman Mudd still tried to vindicate Aleister Crowley's name.

At this time Luck intervened on Crowley's behalf. He was in Paris with Dorothy Olsen and also Leah and Mudd, when he was contacted by Heinrich Tranker from Hohenleuben in Thiringia, Germany. Tranker was the OTO, Grand Master for Germany but he wished to set up his own Order which he eventually did; The Pansophic Lodge of the Light Seeking Brethern of the Orient. He paid Crowley's debts in Paris and the fares for the four of them to travel to Germany. Leah and Mudd made their home there with Martha Kuntzel a member of the Order. Leah had another child whom she called Al and lived at Martha's lodgings in Leipzig. Her other child had been taken back to America by her sister. Martha Kuntzel was a friend of Madame Lavatsky the Mystic and Theosophist. Leah wrote to Crowley and renounced her role as Scarlet Woman, a clear indication that she was cutting him out of her Life. John Symonds tells us that she was the woman, of all the women that he had known, that came closest to his heart. She returned to America in the 1930s and became a Roman Catholic which gave her some peace. Norman Mudd drowned himself on 16th June 1934 in Guernsey at Portelet Bay. He was an MA and Professor of Applied Mathematics at Grey University College, Bloemfontein, South Africa. He had been living in a Lodging House in Camden Town, London NW1. He was the Guide, Philosopher and friend of Aleister Crowley.

KARL JOHANNES GERMER OF WEIDA, GERMANY
AND FRATER ACHAD'S DEMISE

Karl Germer was a member of The Pansophic Lodge of the Light Seeking Brethern of the Orient. Germer was attracted to Crowley's sex magic as he had problems sexually with sexual function, pleasure and orgasm. In fact his erotic fantasies were of invisibility, escape and hermaphroditism. His marriage to his wife Maria was difficult to say the least, due to these problems.

The Pansophic Lodge had a publishing wing and that same year issued 7 titles. Three of them were by Crowley; this was an alchemical marriage and perhaps a marriage made in heaven. It should be mentioned here that Germer would later be imprisoned by the Nazis and then forced to leave Germany. A member of this Lodge Martha Kuntzel became the standard bearer of Thelema in Germany, and embraced Hitler and Nazi Ideology. She died during World War II. However prior to this she formed the Verlag Press in Leipzig helped by Otto Gebhardi.

Though Crowley hoped to win Tranker over to Thelema he found this to be a losing game. Increasingly he spent more time with Germer and finally moved to Weida in Autumn 1925.

Weida

During this Autumn he was also waging War on Charles Jones also known as Frater Achad, in Chicago. Crowley accused Frater Achad of meglomania and the theft of books and manuscripts. As is well known Crowley was often accusing colleagues and ex-colleagues of theft. 'Chac'un son gout' as the French say! However he had heard that Charles Jones had gone mad. The strain of his role as Grade Master of the Temple had been too much for him. Jones came to England for a time and joined the Roman Catholic Church. For some reason he thought that he could convert members of the Catholic Faith to Thelema. This did not work and he returned to Vancouver and was found wandering naked in the streets. Crowley felt he had ascended too quickly from the grade of Neophyte to Master of the Temple. Eventually though Jones recovered. He pronounced Aiwass, Crowley's Guardian Angel as a malignant Intelligence. His belief now was that the New Aeon was from the Goddess Maat, the Goddess of Wisdom & Justice - not Horus. When Crowley heard that Jones had turned against him he invoked demons to destroy him. In 1936 he expelled him from the OTO.

Crowley returned to Tunisia briefly with Dorothy Olsen in November 1925. Leahs' son Alexander Barron-Hirsig was born in Leipzig in December 1925. Certainly Crowley could see that things were coming to an end. He moved to Paris in 1926 and rented a flat at 55 Avenue de Suffren. During 1926 and 1927 he acquired a series of mistresses - John Symonds tells us eight in all. The last of these Margaret Binetti he denounced for her 'callous heartlessness and hypocritical falsity'. Which brings me back to the Law of Perpetual Motion again.

Avenue de Suffren

In 1926 Crowley had a new disciple, one Thomas Driberg who was at Christ Church College, Oxford. Driberg had written to Crowley in November 1925 and he was precisely the kind of student Crowley liked, well-heeled and upper-middle class. Driberg mentions Crowley in his memoirs published in 1977, called 'Ruling Passions'. Although a great hope for Crowley's fortunes Dribergs' professing in letters to be devoted to magic, came to nothing. He was an ambitious man and in later life he was a member of the Labour Party's National Executive and a closet homosexual. Driberg mentioned about Crowley in the 1920s "He claimed to have learned wisdom from the Secret Masters in Tibet. This wisdom may have included certain formulae for sexual potency, for though he was bisexual, I was to observe over the years that, ugly as he was, he could exercise a compelling fascination over women, particularly elderly women with a fair amount of money".

It was also in 1926 that Jane Wolfe visited Crowley and Dorothy Olsen in La Marsa and wrote that she felt Dorothy Olsen showed manic-depressive patterns and often drank. Dorothy Olsen complained to Jane that Crowley has "run around with Arab boys in Sidi-bou Said....he almost killed me once when we were out in the desert.... An arab boy came to me weeping and saying 'I don't want him, I don't want him'...." Dorothy was clearly jealous of Crowley's male lovers. She left him on his birthday, 12th October 1926. He was 51 years old At this time a film was being shot in Nice of The Magician written by Somerset Maugham. The lead character Oliver Haddo was based on Crowley and it was directed by Rex Ingram. Unfortunately it was slated by critics in 1927 and died a death.

Crowley wrote a poem called Gigolomastix in Paris in December 1926. He was looking for a new lover, really a new Scarlet Woman and also had thoughts on marrying again. His poem goes like this:-
"If I was just a Pekinese
I'd have some fat old greasy sow
To pet me, comb me, catch my fleas
See to my comfort and my chow
Thank God, although I starve and freeze
That I am not a Pekinese!"

Crowley had one or two brief affairs with men at this time too. One such was Louis Eugene de Cayenne in Paris. He was also receiving financial support from Karl Germer who was living in Paris. However another American friend sent a well-to-do Polish woman to see him, Kasimira Bass. Kasimira wrote back to Wilfred T Smith, their mutual friend that Crowley, "has a nice place on the outskirts of Paris, a Jap butler, and a female housekeeper. He received me with attention at the door and served me a cocktail called 'Maya' as strong as himself. We chatted and smoked fine cigarettes and after half an hour he took me to some funny people in a studio for dinner. He loves, as you know, adventures and he likes to observe the lives of unbalanced human beings... We talked until 3am...He proposed to me 4 times!"
Crowley wrote to Wilfred T Smith to thank him, "... for the galleon of Treasure which came under full sail into port here last week....." Bass went on to Poland and joined Crowley once again in the Winter of 1928 at Fountainebleau. However their relationship came to nothing and in December 1928 she had returned to America.

Crowley was, in fact, engaged at this time to someone called Cora Eaton; a middle aged and middle class American woman. She was of modest means but fell deeply in love with Germer. Germer was fond of her though could not return her passion. Crowley, however insisted that they should marry and that Cora should fund his publication efforts with $10,000. Cora didn't have this much money but instead gave him $6500, even though she had severe doubts about Crowley at this time. However, Cora and Germer were married in June 1929.

CROWLEY'S NEW FOLLOWERS - 1928

An important new friend and disciple of this period is Gerald Yorke whose home was at Forthampton Court above. He had attended Eton and Cambridge, and could have had a good business career. However he loved Crowley's writings and travelled to Paris to meet him in late 1927. Yorke was tolerant of Crowley who he called 'the Old Sinner' and stayed friends with him til the end of his life. Yorke however was canny and never completely committed to Thelema or to everything Crowley asked of him. Gerald Yorke had spiritual ardour and a good business head with which he aided Crowley later in his life.

Gerald Yorke

Israel Regardie came to Paris on Crowley's 53rd birthday, 12th October 1928. He had been corresponding with the Great Beast for some years. Israel was the son of poor Jewish immigrants from the East End of London. They had emigrated to America where Israel had attended Art College in Philadelphia and wanted to become a painter. He was influenced by Madame Blavatsky's writings at fifteen and developed an interest for the esoteric. Because of Crowley's reputation Israel told his parents that he was going off to study Art in Paris. Crowley introduced the young and virginal Israel to sex almost straight away in

Madame Helena Blavatsky - the Mystic

Paris, a shocking beginning to his Thelemite learning. He also suggested that he frequent prostitutes and asked him to hand over all his money. When Israel went to London, Crowley sent him to his tailors in Jermyn Street and told him to order himself a good suit and send the bill to Crowley, which Israel did. Crowley supported him when he was stuck in Brussels for some months and could not get back into England. Eventually Regardie was allowed in.

Israel Regardie

It is in 1929 that we find out that Crowley was friendly with Montague Summers who wrote 'The History of Witchcraft and Demonology'. Summers was a typical British eccentric and a knowlegeable man. He believed in the Devil and the accusations made against women as witches during the Inquisition. Crowley had dinner with him on 5th July 1929 and noted " Dinner with Monty Summers! The most amusing evening I have spent in decades", indicating respect and good feeling between the two friends. Summers took a lot of interest in Crowley and had a large portfolio of press cuttings and magazines articles on him. He spoke of Crowley as ' one of the few original and really interesting men of our age'.

Montague Summers, formerly a Roman Catholic Priest

It was at this time that Gerald Yorke offered to partly fund a print of 'Magick in Theory and Practice' - through the Lecram Press in Paris. Crowley also had plans to publish 'Moonchild' and 'Confessions' at this time. He hired a publicity agent Vidal Hunt in Paris who he had met some years before. However Crowley would not comply with the wishes of this publicity agent and their relationship ended antagonistically. Hunt went to the Police with stories of Crowley's dealings and so is likely to have been threatened by him. Crowley realised he wanted to remain peacefully in France. At the end of 1928 he met Maria Teresa de Miramar who was to become his next Scarlet Woman.
These nomadic years of wandering in France and in North Africa whilst still on heroin and other drugs had taken their toll on aging Aleister Crowley. Unable to survive without a relationship and constantly pushing for publication of his works whilst making no compromise to publishers or benefactors left him lonely and disillusioned. La Belle Epoque was behind him and he was no longer the young, attractive, entertaining and daring Magician and bonne viveur. He was the Crowley of 'The Great Beast,' who the Sunday Express had called 'The Wicked Man in the World!'. He was Perdurabo in exile, still trying to make a name for himself and still living on small legacies and handouts. How had the mighty fallen. The loyalty of Yorke and the devotion of Regardie was sorely needed at this time.

The police called on Crowley on 17th January 1929, seemingly due to his publishing 'Magick in Theory and Practice'. This was not in fact published until 12 April 1929 but word was out it was in the pipeline. Maria Del Miramar with whom he now was in a relationship protested to the Nicaraguan Consul about harassment as she was from Nicaragua. However Crowley was no longer welcome in France and his friends Maria and Israel Regardie were asked to leave also. Crowley took to his bed due to illness. Maria del Miramar and Israel left for England. Crowley was lambasted as a German Spy based on his World War One activities and his membership of the German OTO by 'Paris Midi'. Israel Regardie and Maria del Miramar were refused permission to land in England and had to go to Brussels. There Regardie was seduced by Del Miramar, who may have wearied of Crowley at the time. Or may simply have been bored and lonely.

Maria del Miramar and Aleister Crowley

Maria del Miramar was a strong character and could drink heavily. She had been born in Granada, Nicaragua; her mother was French and her Father Italian. She was attractive and exotic to Crowley and it was no wonder that he married her, at age thirty four. In February 1929 she was accosted by Kasimira Bass on board a bus, probably through jealousy. Crowley was with her and she stood up to Bass, being used to turbulence in relationships. Certainly the relationship she had with Crowley was full of scenes and unsettled but she carried on throughout with him.

Crowley held out in France until 12th April 1929 when 'Magick in Theory and Practice' was published; with the help of a doctor's certificate for ill health. He then travelled to Brussels on 17th April where he again met Maria del Miramar and consummated a passionate and sexual reunion. It was at this time that they decided to marry. In late May, Crowley travelled to England and his fare was paid by a Colonel Carter of Scotland Yard, a friend of Gerald Yorke's. Crowley had been worried that he would be pilloried or prosecuted by the authorities but this did not happen. However he was persona non grata in the eyes of the publishing world. Publisher Rupert Grayson had this to say about Crowley: "Crowley the Black Magician had propelled his drug charged body to see us................I was truly revolted........When he left the room I opened the windows and doors to rid the room of the atmosphere of aromatic evil he had left....it was the only book I remember turning down for no better reason than our instant dislike for its author". Prejudice and bigotry such as this meant that Crowley had little chance with publishers without great help. He found this help when he called on P R Stephenson, the editorial director of the newly founded Mandrake Press in June 1929.

The Mandrake Press was owned by Edward Goldston, a rare book dealer. That same month they had published 'The Paintings of D H Lawrence', whose notoriety over 'Lady Chatterley's Lover' was very recent.. The London exhibition of these paintings held in conjunction with the book being published was raided by the Police! Aleister Crowley was right up their street. They advanced him £50. Mandrake then published, The Strategem, Moonchild, and also Confessions in September 1929.

THE PRODIGAL SON RETURNS TO THE HOME OF HIS FOREFATHERS

Knockholt, Kent

Crowley came home to Kent, the County known as the Garden of England. He had married Maria del Miramar on 16th August 1929 in Leipzig with the British Consul in attendance. He was determined to come back to England with her and to make a go of their marriage. In many ways it was his last hope for a more stable life. However this was not to be. As with his first wife Maria drank heavily. She began to suffer from paranoia and also had a vile temper making accusations that Crowley and her Nurse were trying to poison her. Crowley had taken her to Ivy Cottage in Knockholt feeling that a quiet countryside environment would help calm and settle her. Unfortunately this did not work. The symptoms she expressed would indicate alcoholism and must surely have reminded him of his marriage to Rose Kelly. The couple spent the Winter of 1929 to 1930 in relative isolation. P R Stephenson lived nearby in Kent and must have helped him find the cottage. He was working on a book called 'The Legend of Aleister Crowley' which was to expose and refute the Press Campaign against Crowley. Israel Regardie was allowed into England at this time and was to assist Stephenson in this; he was credited as a co-author in 1970 when their work was republished. A new company, The Mandrake Press Ltd was founded in March 1930. It was funded partly by Cora Germer who put in £500. Even when things were so difficult Crowley and another director Thynne were too free with the funds. Crowley seemed unable to realise that economy was needed at this early stage of the Press and spent wildly on lunches and dinners and other extravagances.

Controversy still followed Crowley wherever he went. He was asked to give a talk at Oxford University Poetry Society in February 1930. One of those who was fascinated by Crowley's presence was Arthur Calder-Marshall. However the Oxford authorities led by a Roman Catholic Priest, Father Ronald Knox threatened severe sanctions should Crowley be allowed to lecture. Fortunately this incident was seen as useful to the businessman Stephenson. He had 1000 copies of the lecture text printed as a 16 page pamphlet, 'The Banned Lecture, Gilles de Rais'. The newspapers in Oxford covered this controversy with relish and sales of the pamphlet were brisk. This matter must have been remembered in Oxford some 14 or 15 years later when Lady Frieda Harris wanted to hold an exhibition of the Tarot Card paintings she and Crowley had produced during the Second World War. But that is some years ahead.

Magick in Principle and Practice was again published in the Summer of 1930 by the Mandrake Press Ltd. Victor Neuberg reviewed it for The Sunday Referee in October 1930. He wrote, "The writer's accomplishment is patent; he is a master, at any rate, of prose. His power of expression is as near perfect as that of any author I have read". Neuberg perhaps was seeking a reconciliation with Crowley and if this is so Crowley was very pleased with the review. Sadly the Mandrake Press Ltd fell into bankruptcy in November 1930. There was no reconciliation with Neuberg.

AC in literary pose

REPUTATION AND CAREER

Published at Last

The trigram that represents Career and Reputation is Kan
It is in the Later Heaven Arrangement of trigrams and its direction is North. For Crowley, in his personal Pa Tzu compass - this was the direction of Disagreements. I have always felt that the Rock in Cefalu must be in this direction and it had an overbearing effect on Crowley and those residing at the Abbey. K'an represents Water. It is dangerous and fearless full of hidden perils and swirling erosive forces according to the I Ching. Its animal is the Pig or Boar and it is lacking in great strength, tending to be soft and spongy and soaking up water.

Kan symbolises the Cold of Winter and the danger or opportunity of Water. It can represent illusions like the reflection of the Moon on Water - or great success; but only through the person hiding their strength and appearing weak. It represents situations of entanglement and a perpetual position of danger. An example of this would be through court intrigues at the Emperor's court by the mandarins. One false step and death could result. For Career and Reputation or Fame this was not an area to take lightly for Crowley. The North could be Boleskine House, Leamington Spa, London and other Northerly locations. Having worked out Crowley's Kua number, which is a 7, it is seen that West was the best direction for him and his Career. As can be seen, in respect to America, this has proven to be the case.

Lillian Too tells us that, "Houses and buildings built too near graveyards, hospitals, prisons, slaughter-houses and police stations are too yin because such places are associated with the yin energies of death. Even places of workship, such as temples, abbeys, churches and mosques are said to give out extreme yin energies because of the rituals associated with mourning held there. The same diagnosis is often pronounced on buildings that are located on land that previously housed these places, making it advisable to research the history of such a home".
Of Water the Tao Te Ching says:-
"Rivers and the sea are able to rule the streams of
One hundred valleys

Because they are good at taking the lower position
The streams of a hundred valleys run to them
Therefore, if you want to rule effectively over people
You must surely speak as if below them
If you want to lead well
You must surely walk behind them
That way when the Sage takes a position of Power
The people will not feel oppressed
And when the Sage leads
The people will not think that he is in the Way
Therefore the whole world joyfully praises him
And does not tire of him
Because he refuses to compete
The World cannot compete with him".

Crowley eventually learnt this in Life. But not yet. His head was too busy scheming and analysing to understand the way of the Tao. Though this would happen in time.

In his book Tao Te Ching, Lao Tzu, he wrote,
"The Concealment of Light: Heaven and Earth are mighty in continuance, because their work is delivered from the Lust of Result. Thus also the Sage, seeking not any goal, attaineth all things; he doth not interfere in the affairs of his body, and so that body acteth without friction. It is because he meddleth not with personal aims, that these come to pass with simplicity".

Spirit Gates

Crowley was now at the height of his notoriety. There were many stories and rumours floating about concerning him. One such concerns the Watkins Bookshop in London, so John Symonds tells us in The Great Beast. " John Watkins invited Crowley to demonstrate his Magick when he was visiting the occult bookshop one day. 'Close your Eyes' said AC. John Watkins did so. When he opened them again all his books had vanished from the shelves! Crowley was nowhere to be seen either!"

Another Urban Legend is that whenever Crowley entered the Café Royale a silence fell over everyone and no one dared to speak until Crowley had been seated. On another occasion we find a note from his diary when travelling in Germany, "Arose in my Might and stopped the gramophone in the Terminus by threatening all present with immediate death!" Crowley, smelling of strong oils such as ambergris and musk had a profound effect on those he came into contact with. He appearance, strong staring eyes in a fat face, shaved head and eccentric and unusual dress presented a strong aura.

The real Aleister Crowley

It is extraordinary that Crowley learnt nothing from his difficult relationships and marriages with women. He adored Maria del Miramar and was very attracted to her when he first met her. He set her up on a pedestal and called her his glorious Scarlet Woman. Much was asked of her emotionally, spiritually and magically as was Crowley's way. He behaved with cutting disdain and dismissal when relationships fell apart or his women could not live up to his expectations. Rose Kelly, Dorothy Olsen and Maria del Miramar all seemed to fall into alchoholism and Leah Hirsig became ill and addicted to drugs. He was picking the same kind of women who wanted an adventurous time and were interested in travel and taking risks. Yet all were emotionally frail and needed support. Crowley got them to walk a tightrope and they often fell. It is clear that with Maria del Miramar he tried to make a go of the marriage and to offer her some support by taking her to a quiet English village such as Knockholt and spending time with her. In April 1930 they visited Berlin in order to organise an exhibition of his paintings. The Weimar Republic was a permissive society with openly gay and bisexual nightclubs such as Christopher Isherwood described in his work 'Carbaret'. Crowley relished this environment and the avant guarde. Stephen Spender was also in Berlin at this time. Crowley met a painter called Steiner who was helping him to organise his exhibition and he was interviewed in the Berliner Tageblatt.

Whilst visiting Steiner's studio that April, with Maria del Miramar, he met Hanni Larissa a young artist of 19. Crowley found in her a gaunt beauty and was captivated. He wrote in his diary that he was in love with her and this marked the end of his marriage. Crowley and Maria returned to England and in June 1930 moved to 89 Park Mansions in Knightsbridge. I know these mansion flats because they are above a row of shops and near to Harvey Nichols today. They are in a very affluent part of town, then as now and would be costly to rent.

Park Mansions, Knightsbridge

Crowley and Maria were not happy in this home and he complained that she was often drunk, flirting with male visitors and prone to violent scenes. He further complained to anyone who would listen, that she made little effort to learn English. With the marriage in tatters he decided to run away again and returned to Germany in August 1930. From Germany he contacted solicitors to dissolve the marriage. He never saw Maria del Miramar again.

Gerald Yorke ended up helping Maria, finding her a small flat in Hampstead. He wrote that Crowley " had left his wife penniless and without support in London. I kept back what little money I had of his and doled it out to her. At the same time I refused to have further dealings with him". But Crowley was on to the next woman, Hanni Jaeger who he immediately bedded that same August. Crowley embarked on sexual rituals with Hanni to give them both energy and health, yet both of them suffered bouts of illness during the time they were together.
Plus sa Change! Plus sa meme Change!

In August 1930 Aleister Crowley and Hanni Jaeger left Berlin for Lisbon in Portugal. This was a trip to cement their relationship but it was also at the invitation of Fernando Pessoa an acclaimed Poet and leading figure in the Modernist Movement in Portugal. Pessoa was translating the 'Hymn to Pan', Crowley's poem, into Portuguese, he once wrote " I am a nomadic wanderer through my consciousness". It was a wonderful and positive trip for Crowley and for Pessoa, especially in regard to publicity. Crowley had decided to pretend to commit suicide in Portugal and thereby raise attention for his books. He asked Pessoa to collude with him in this and Pessoa agreed with alacrity.

Crowley & Pessoa playing Chess in a café in Lisbon

The place chosen for the fake suicide was the coastal town of Cascais with its tourist attraction of the Boca do Infierno (Mouth of Hell), a tunnel-shaped cliff face which had been battered by the wind and waves of the Atlantic ocean. Hanni Jaeger and Crowley found a hotel near to this and he seduced her into several days of sexual gymnastics. Hanni was very upset after these 3 days and quarrelled ferociously with Crowley. The Hotel Manager asked them to leave and thus Hanni fled to Lisbon. Crowley followed Hanni and engaged her in sexual magic with the object of continuing their relationship. However this did not work and Hanni Jaeger fled from Crowley and left for Germany. She was still only 19, whilst Crowley was 55.

Crowley returned to Boca do Infierno on 21st September and wrote in his diary, "I decide to do suicide stunt and annoy Hanni, Arrange details with Pessoa".

Boca do Infierno

The press in London, Paris and Lisbon gave coverage to this incident. A suicide note from Crowley was found along with his cigarette case, above the rock. The suicide note read, "I cannot live without thee. The other Mouth of Hell will catch me. I will not be as hot as thine. Hisos. Tu Li Yu" This was printed in The Empire News. The Portuguese police noted that a man answering Crowley's description had left the country 2 days later. Hanni Jaeger had sent a telegram of reconciliation to Crowley and he had travelled to join her in Berlin.

Once in Germany Crowley sought to continue friendships with the literary community. In October 1930 he dined with J W N Sullivan who introduced Crowley to Aldous Huxley. Another myth about Crowley, regarding Aldous Huxley is that Crowley introduced Huxley to mescaline which later lead to Huxley's writing 'The Doors of Perception' in 1954. This is completely untrue as mescaline was not around in Berlin at this time. Crowley however did paint a portrait of Huxley.

Aldous Huxley in 1930

Crowley remained in Berlin until June 1932. He pursued sexual relationships with both men and women at this time. He did however remain with Hanni but was restless due to his dependence on Karl and Cora Germer. Cora was annoyed at Crowley's lifestyle and extravagance; his demands on her and Karl were also causing hardship. The Depression had arrived and depleted Cora's savings. Germer was torn between his wife and his Master. In November 1930 Hanni accused Germer of forcing her to observe whilst he masturbated in a toilet. Crowley was furious and wrote in his diary, "Karl is a filthy, asexual maniac..!" But there were many sexual games at this time between Crowley and Hanni so this may have been untrue. Their relationship declined in January 1931 and Hanni left him for a time. They reconciled and then both became ill. Hanni was pregnant but sadly miscarried and may have been using drugs too. Crowleys' interest in her declined.

Berlin 1931; Crowley entered a promiscuous phase with a number of women. He wrote to Gerald Yorke that he was unlikely to come to England unless he was paid to do so. His sexual posturing though, could no longer masquerade as Magick and he continued to create emotional and sexual dramas with his lovers. He was stuck in a time warp from his youth and avoiding returning to England where he would have to face the decline of his marriage and any subsequent divorce. Del Miramar, or Mrs Crowley was in dire straits emotionally and financially. Crowley had offered her a divorce, however he would also have to pay his ex-wife something from the family trust fund administered by George Cecil Jones and Gerald Yorke.

The drug addiction, to heroin, cocaine and drinking were taking their toll on Crowley. He was on a merry-go-round and a road to nowhere, at the same time. The patterns of his relationships with women were stark. They were lasting now for a matter of weeks or months. He had no patience or compassion and was out of money and out of ideas. Magick occupied him less and the flight into hedonism more. He was on a collision course and it was a matter of not whether but when. Friends were providing a safety net for him but he was rapidly running out of friends. How long before he was financially and morally bankrupt? Much of this lifestyle at this time is described in his novel 'Diary of a Drug Fiend'. The merry-go-round of Sir Peter Pendragon and his wife, mirror this era in early 1930s Berlin.

Colonel Carter of Scotland Yard wrote to Crowley to come back from the Continent and look after his wife probably at the behest of Gerald Yorke. Crowley wrote back with indifference. He would do nothing. A month later she was admitted to Colney Hatch Mental Hospital in June 1931 just as Rose Kelly had been. Crowley provided some information as to her background to the hospital and she remained there for over 30 years. She died there and never did divorce Aleister Crowley. When he died he was still married to her in 1947.

Colney Hatch Mental Hospital - today gentrified as apartments.

STRANGE DAYS IN DECADANT BERLIN 1931

Café Wintergarten, Berlin 1930

Inevitably, Crowley picked up another woman to erase the immediate past relationship and the demise of his wife. Ever the escapologist, Crowley met Bertha Busch on 3rd August 1931. Her nickname was 'Billie'. Billie was gaunt and in poor physical health, as his previous women had been. She was also prone to outbursts of melancholy, probably due to her excessive drinking. The hallmarks of an addict seeking his counterpart in excessive indulgence, were revealed in Crowleys' declaration of love for Bertha Busch. He declared her his Scarlet Woman and moved into a flat with her at 2, Karlsruhestrasse in Berlin. The funds for this were provided by Germer.

As luck would have it the Galerie Neumann-Neirendorf in Berlin agreed to put on an exhibition of 73 of Crowley's paintings during October and November 1931. They drew attention; some paintings were from New York some from Cefalu, others were completed in Berlin. There were portraits of Aldous Huxley, Leah Hirsig, Norman Mudd, J W N Sullivan, Maria del Miramar and Helena Blavatsky, amongst others. Though today these paintings reach high prices there is no record of any being sold at this exhibition. However Crowley was popular amongst the British in Berlin at this time because of this publicity. He entertained the likes of Christopher Isherwood and Stephen Spender - and continued his indulgence of heroin and cocaine.

Stephen Spender

Christopher Isherwood reflected on his acquaintance with Crowley some years later, "The truly awful thing about Crowley is that one suspects that he didn't really believe in anything. Even his wickedness. Perhaps the only thing that wasn't fake was his addiction to heroin and cocaine". How clearly the perusal of this Life, through the path he has taken, shows Crowley's descent into Hell, the hell of addiction, and thereby the road to failure. A brilliant mind, a clever man, recognised by other clever men and women, once a shining light, which had almost gone out.

Crowley was befriended at this time by Gerald Hamilton. He was the model for 'Mr Norris' in Christopher Isherwood's novel, 'Mr Norris Changes Trains'. Isherwood had immortalised Crowley in a story he wrote called, 'A Visit to Anselm Oakes' from a book called Exhumations. Gerald Yorke had asked Gerald

Hamilton to take some English money to Berlin and give it to Crowley. This he did; it was £50. It was the same £50 which Scotland Yard were paying Crowley for reporting to them on Gerald Hamilton's left wing activities. At the same time Gerald Hamilton was receiving sums from British Intelligence for reporting on Crowley's activities. Wheels within wheels!

Hamilton stayed with Crowley and Bertha Busch during January and February 1932. He was therefore witness to Crowley and Billie's stormy rows and plate-throwing relationship. Eventually Billie stabbed the Beast just below the shoulder blade and he was badly weakened in December 1931. A doctor had to be called and Crowley lost a lot of blood. He now realised that even his indulgences, women or drugs, were no longer life enhancing but rather, life changing and even perhaps life ending. So at this time Crowley drew up his will and made Gerald Yorke his executor.

Crowley sent Bertha Busch to London to see Gerald Yorke in May 1932 when he needed money. It was not forthcoming. He was evicted from the flat on 22nd June and was therefore compelled to return to London.

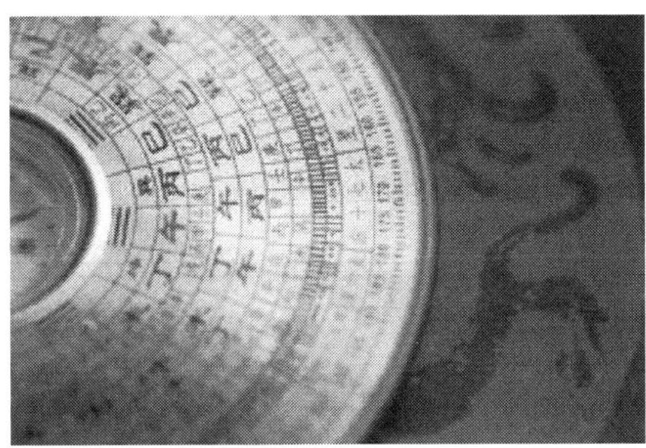

POVERTY AND SOUR GRAPES

Crowley was now dependent on the kindness of friends and connections. To anyone else that would have meant using tact and diplomacy or at least becoming more contrite. Crowley refused to recognise the reality of his predicament. He was poor. But like a gambler he constantly had an eye on the next book deal, the next painting sale, the next gullible woman to step in his path. Friends enabled him to rent a flat at 27 Albemarle Street in Central London. He began again to contact publishers who might be interested in his work 'Confessions', and a book of his experiences in Berlin.

Apartments above 26 - 27 Albemarle Street

Israel Regardie, his student had now become a published author in London and had managed to get his work on Magick accepted by a publishing house. He had also moved on from Crowley and become a member of the Order of the Golden Dawn. In 1932 Regardie had had 2 books published, 'A Garden of Pomegranates' and 'The Tree of Life'; both were influenced by Crowley's teachings. In 1937 he sent Crowley a copy of another book he had had published, with a friendly note. Crowley replied with a resentful letter. This was the beginning of an enmity between Regardie and Crowley. That Autumn Crowley circulated an anonymous and libellous letter about Regardie. Israel Regardie was very angry but as the years passed he mellowed. He came to see Crowley for who he was and to forgive him. Regardie died in 1985 but said of Crowley before he passed, "Everything I am today, I owe to him!".

That July in 1932 Crowley went to visit his wife, Maria del Miramar in Colney Hatch Mental Hospital. He wanted her to sign a document that would agree to a divorce and waive any claims for a settlement. However her doctors advised that he not see her, and stated that her case was hopeless. For some strange reason he took Bertha Busch with him. Perhaps to show Maria that he wished

to remarry. Bertha created a scene in the street afterwards and thereby sealed her fate. She and Crowley would soon part; the writing was on the wall, again.
In September 1932 Crowley was invited to a literary luncheon by Christina Foyle. Christina Foyle owned Foyle's bookshop in London and held a literary lunch every year. This was a small coup for Crowley, to be invited as the guest of honour and speaker. Crowley spoke on The Philosophy of Magick which was well received. A queue of women formed at the end of the luncheon to have him autograph their books.

Christina Foyle

This was an Autumn of talks and on 5th October 1932 Crowley delivered another to the National Laboratory of Psychical Research called 'The Elixir of Life: Our Magical Medicine'. The person who had asked him to speak was none other than Harry Price, a famous researcher of paranormal phenomena. Crowley this time stopped short of describing sex magic. He was building a new and better reputation, though the publicity was not as great as his talk in Oxford had been.
At this time Gerald Yorke set off for China and the Far East. He had realised that Crowley would always survive, one way or another. Crowley had begun legal action against him for mismanagement of literary properties and financial assets. He sent a writ to Yorke for £40,000; a friend and supporter to Crowley and his wife for many years. Luckily for Yorke, Crowley had no money to pursue this legal action. With Yorke leaving, all of his friends had left him and his relationship with Bertha Busch was in its end stages. In February 1933 Crowley took a new lover, Marianne, from Bulgaria. He took other women as lovers too in order to perform sex magic and to rejuvenate his energies. Thus he sought to offset his asthma and bronchitis also as he was approaching 60.
In April 1933, Nancy Cunard, an old friend, invited Crowley to contribute to something she was writing on behalf of the 'Scottsboro Boys'. These were 9 young black men falsely accused of raping 2 white women, in Alabama. Crowley made a statement and also wrote, "this case is typical of the hysterical sadism of the American people - the result of Puritanism, and the climate!". He attended a demonstration on behalf of the 'Scottsboro Boys' on 10th April.

CAN THE LAW BE USED TO DEFEND MAGICK?

Shortly after 1933 began Crowley was in Paddington, West London. He wandered down Praed Street and looked in a bookshop window. There, on this cold January 7th day, he saw his own book 'Moonchild' for sale. This might have been gratifying had he not seen with it a note from the bookseller, "Aleister Crowley's First Novel 'The Diary of a Drug Fiend' was withdrawn from circulation after an attack in the sensational press".

Crowley was furious as this was not true and wrote in his diary , "Discovered libel at 23 Praed Street". He immediately spoke to his lawyer. The case was tried on May 10th, so John Symonds informs us and heard by a Mr Justice Bennett. Bennett advised "There was not the smallest ground for suggesting that any book Mr Crowley had written was indecent or improper. Mr Gray, the bookseller wanted the public to believe that the book to which the label was attached was an indecent book". Crowley was awarded £50 damages plus costs.

In August 1933, Crowley met Pearl Brooksmith who was 35 and not at all rich. He consulted the I Ching on whether to get involved with her nor not and received what he perceived to be a positive reply. Within days he had consummated his union with this new Scarlet Woman and lit a fire which she drew towards. "I feel the flame of fornication creeping up my body", she told him. Buoyed up by this new relationship and his success in the courts Crowley looked for someone else to sue.

An artist he knew, Nina Hamnett had written a book 'Laughing Torso' about her experiences when visiting Cefalu. Although she wrote and told Crowley that there was nothing libellous in her book, Crowley wasn't so sure. On reading it he found out that he had a temple; 'he was supposed to practice Black Magic there and one day a baby mysteriously disappeared. There was a goat there too, and the inhabitants of the village were frightened of him'. Crowley went to see his lawyer but he had not the concrete evidence he had had with Mr Gray. Also Crowley had been friends with Nina Hamnett for 20 years. This could have been settled out of court. Constable and Co, her publishers were a large concern and opposed him. Old friends and acquaintances would not testify in court as to his good character and his lawyer advised against challenging this large publishers. But when had Crowley listened to anyone's sound advice?

The case opened on 10th April 1934 in the High Court. Crowley's beliefs and past behaviour were openly questioned and exposed. This was no longer a libel trial but rather a trial of Aleister Crowley and his Life and Magical rituals. On the fourth day, after 3 days of damning evidence against AC the Judge asked the Jury if they needed to hear much more. They didn't, and returned a verdict for the defendants, Nina Hamnett and her publishers. Crowley was indeed crushed and left court almost too emotional to speak.

A Top Hat to Court

Crowley had destroyed his friendship with Nina Hamnett who was a talented painter and had once worked for Crowley as a muralist at his flat at 124 Victoria Street, near Victoria Station. In fact it was Nina Hamnett who first discovered the body of Joan Hayes also known as Ione de Forest, and Victor Neuberg's mistress. Crowley after this trial claimed to have been to bed with Nina Hamnett and was uncomplimentary about her. In fact this was not true and they had never been lovers. But those days were now gone and after the libel case there was no warmth left between them. Nina Hamnett died in 1956 and it is rumoured that she had committed suicide due to a curse cast on her by Crowley. But Crowley had been dead for 9 years. Nina wrote in her book, a caption, "Aleister Crowley who started the fun and games at the Law Courts in 1934". Next to this she outlined a small drawing!

Nina Hamnett

OUT OF THE TAO EMERGES THE ONE

The Journey of Feng Shui is inextricably linked to the Way of the Tao. One has to become like water and to flow. The self discipline needed in order for Life to flow and therefore for Life to expand is one acquired through the process of meditation and ritual discipline. Crowley as a young man and young magician had begun this process and Life started to develop for him particularly when he was living at 124 Victoria Street SW1. Of course Life throws obstacles at us and we deal with those as best we can but on the whole he was on track. His asthma and drug addiction were his worst enemies and he was ill advised on both. Travelling to America brought new horizons and new contacts but increasingly he failed to learn from personal experience. As the drugs caught hold he lost all perspective save for money and physical indulgence.

Conventional logic dissolves in the Tao Te Ching. Crowley knew this in his head but not in his heart which is why he could not completely surrender to its wisdom. If he could have, he would have been able to leave heroin and cocaine behind and lead a more aesthetic life, of simplicity and spiritual or magical beliefs devoid of Desire - Samsara - as the Buddhists say. This is why he loved the I Ching which bases itself on a strict logic of cause and effect. Yet the Tao Te Ching sees connections between apparently unrelated phenomena. It is not simply the Law of opposites as Crowley seems to assume in his book on Lao Tsu; interesting and poetic though it is. Mirrors are important in Feng Shui. Yet on a deeper level they lead you to more profound observations of how you see yourself and your World, letting in light and illuminating different areas of your Life.

Interestingly we are told that the number 7, which is Crowley's Pa Kua number corresponds to Metal and to West and the trigram Lake as previously mentioned. This trigram pattern is often known as 'sharp energy' and can either increase a person's power in certain types of conflict or bring about harm, such as an apparent accident with a sharp knife. One is reminded of the battle with Bertha Busch. It would have been interesting to perform Feng Shui on the flat at 124 Victoria Street. London SW1.

In 1932 Ethel Archer, Crowleys' old friend from his A:.A:. days published a novel 'The Hieroglyph'. In it she described a Vladimir Svaroff, ie Crowley, Newton was Neuberg and other members of the Silver Star - or A:.A:. She herself is Iris in the novel. Rituals of the Silver Star take place in an apartment in Central London and Ethel describes to us the sitting room at 124 Victoria Street.

"The range of artwork on display was most impressive. Alongside the drawing by Spare was a drawing by Aubrey Beardsley. Above the mantelpiece was a large early Byzantine crucifix of ivory and ebony. Below were figures of the Buddha and of various Egyptian and Chinese Gods, the latter in jade. On top of the bookshelves - which contained first editions of Baudelaire, Swinburne and Wilde, rested busts by Rodin. Another wall featured a silken, embroidered Tibetan scroll. The flat itself was immaculately decorated with bare floors painted black, walls of a sugar-paper blue, with white woodwork and scarlet curtains. The total effect was intoxicating to first time visitors investigating." Thus it was here that Crowley chose to perform The Rites of Eleusis.

Victoria Street London SW1

It is important to report now on an event which occurred as Crowley left the Court on April 13th 1933. A woman approached him called Patricia MacAlpine; she was nineteen. She told him she was outraged by the verdict and that it was totally unjust. Crowley was very emotional at this point and could barely speak. It was then that she offered to have his baby. Such as offering coming at this point was greatly significant and would not have gone unnoticed by the Great Beast. Deidre, which Crowley came to call her, already had two fatherless children. She had a third one by Crowley, a son, who was named Aleister Ataturk, and was very dear to Crowley's heart. The son he had always wanted.

Aleister Crowley and Ataturk

BANKRUPTCY AND ATONEMENT

It was in February 1935 that Aleister Crowley almost 60, entered into voluntary Bankruptcy proceedings; his debts totalling £4695. His assets were nil. Small trust payments, donations from disciples, sporadic gifts from Yorke and other friends were his means now of surviving. Pearl Brooksmith underwent a hysterectomy in January 1936. Her health declined and eventually had to have psychiatric treatment. By May 1936 Crowley recorded that she was constantly suffering from hallucinations. Their relationship was thus, on the decline.

Gerald Yorke returned from his travelling in 1936 and became Crowley's trustee once again. He occasionally gave Crowley gifts of cash but refused to have any other financial dealings with him. So it was to the OTO Agape Lodge in Los Angeles that Crowley now turned for help in getting published. Wilfred T Smith and other members of the Lodge assisted Crowley from now on until the end of his life. The distance between them may well have been an advantage.

In Germany, at around this time Martha Kuntzel tried to place a copy of the Book of the Law in the hands of Adolph Hitler. She had been told by Crowley that the nation that accepted the Law of Thelema would be the first nation of the World. Kuntzel explained that she had been unsuccessful in getting the Book to Hitler. Crowley maintained that somehow a copy of the Book of the Law had been placed with him, though this is unlikely to be true as there is no evidence for this.

Crowley met up again with George Viereck who he had written for in America in his publications, The Fatherland and The International, during World War One. He was pleased that George would sign an affidavit to say that Crowley had no trouble with the authorities in America. Crowley sought from Veireck evidence of his British patriotism and also access to the Fuhrer. So completely Crowley! It is unlikely that Veireck made any moves on Crowley's behalf at this time. The Third Reich had outlawed virtually all esoteric groups which they believed to be under Jewish control, in Germany, including the OTO. The Nazis persecuted Karl Germer and he was arrested in February 1935 on the charge of illegal Masonic connections. Germer was never a Mason but some of the OTO rituals had Masonic symbolism in them. Germer was imprisoned in camps in Berlin and Esterwegen. He said that his Holy Guardian Angel helped and supported him during this period. When he was released Germer wrote to Max Schneider at the OTO Agape Lodge branch. "When the Gestapo were investigating secret societies in general, they discovered my personal relations with Crowley. And it was the secrets of the OTO that they believed to be of supreme political importance. Ever since their ascent to power the Nazis suspected the existence of some secret organisation which wielded some sort of mysterious power and ordered the affairs of the planet. It was from me that they expected to obtain the requisite information. I was exposed to the severest cross-examination and to third degree methods in order to force me to reveal the secrets. Finally I was sent to the terrible Esterwegen Camp with instructions to break me with particular brutality for obstinately refusing to reveal the truth"

Esterwegen Camp , Hanover

Germers' troubles did not end on release. He moved to Belgium but was again arrested and deported to France. He was then interned by the French authorities for several months. Eventually he was allowed to emigrate to America. All of this was due to his links to Crowley. Crowley may have been

critical of Germer but retained a lasting respect for him and his courage, as he held out against the Nazis during this time.
Crowley sought to influence the British Government regarding The Book of the Law. In October 1936, he sent 'Propositions' to the Secretary of War, Alfred Duff Cooper. He argued that military recruitment should be compulsory for both sexes in the face of the Germans gathering might. He felt that the Book of the Law could be useful to the Government in persuading the British public of the necessity of this. However he asked that this be kept secret and to be supported by the 'appropriate services' in its completion.

Crowley sought to influence the Third Reich possibly through his writings in 'The Fatherland' and 'The Internationalist'. Thelema was to be for them the new religion that would justify the master class. Thelema was the ideal framework to exercise power. In the past he had also sought to influence Stalin as well.
He pushed on with his writing and publishing and published 'Book 4 Part IV' at the Autumn Equinox in 1936 to also further the message of Thelema. It had been discussed in the Book of the Law, Chapter 4. "..........Horus...............rules the present period of 2000 years beginning in 1904. Everywhere his government is taking root. Observe for yourselves the decay of the sense of sin, the growth of innocence and irresponsibility, the strange modifications of the reproductive instinct, with a tendency to become bisexual and epicene, the childlike confidence in Progress combined with nightmare fear of Catastrophe, against which we are yet half unwilling to take precautions...........Consider War, the atrocities which occur daily and leave us unmoved and hardly worried. We are children. How this new Aeon of Horus will develop, how the Child will grow up, these are for us to determine, growing up ourselves in the way of the Law of Thelema under the enlightened guidance of the Master Therion".

The first edition of the 'Book of the Law' was only 1000 copies, plus 250 to subscribers, one of whom was George Bernard Shaw. After its publication Crowley had a dream of 4 Adepts, Chinese, Central Asian and 2 others".
As a result on 23 December 1937 he held a ceremony at Cleopatra's Needle on the Embankment in London, to which journalists were invited. There were in attendance representatives of the races of the World, A Jew, An Indian, a Malayan, an African, A Bengali Muslim, and the African was a dancing girl.

Crowley rented a flat in Welbeck Street from 1936-37. His landlord was Alan Burnett-Rae from Oxford; who wrote a book about Crowley's domestic arrangements at this time, stating that he burned large qualtities of incense and had constant rows with Pearl Brooksmith. Eventually Burnett-Rae evicted Crowley for non-payment of rent. They did however, manage to remain cordial. Crowley moved to 6, Hasker Street, where he began a healing practice as a financial concern. He stayed there for 8 months. After this he found new lodgings at 20 Jermyn Street. Then shortly after moved to 24 Chester Terrace, Regents park most probably a more expensive residence.

Chester Gate leading to Chester Terrace

Clever with money, we would have to say, Crowley still managed to live a comfortable lifestyle. He enjoyed magical operations and festive dinners. On 2nd May he held a party for 4 year old Aleister Ataturk in which several ex-lovers were in attendance as well as C R Cammell, Gerald Hamilton and Louis Wilkinson. Two days later he was joined at lunch by Maurice Richardson. Crowley had invited Richardson due to a book review he had written. After this lunch Richardson wrote an article entitled 'My Luncheon with Beast 666'. He wrote, "...when you got used to his eccentricities, and so long as you were not impressed by his mystical pretensions, he was apt to become a fearful bore. He had no capacity for selection, no notion of when to stop. How sinister was he? Obviously he would con a mug, pluck a pigeon". I'm sure you could call Crowley many things but a bore? Journalism had taught Mr Richardson to patronise too, but not to appreciate.

War was declared in September 1939. Crowley wrote to various people to help and support the British war effort. He was introduced to Maxwell Knight, Head of B5 in MI5 by Dennis Wheatley the popular horror novelist and who had written 'The Devil Rides Out'. Both Knight and Wheatley attended rituals with Crowley as background into Wheatley's books. However it was through Naval Intelligence Department that Crowley was almost used as counterintelligence targetting Hitler's Deputy, Rudolph Hess. Hess believed in Astrology and was unsure of the long term prospects for the Third Reich. Ian Fleming, who wrote the James Bond novels felt that Crowley would be useful in infiltrating Hess's circle as a planted MI5 Astrologer. He would convey a fake horoscope. This idea was approved by Maxwell Knight.

Knight had Crowley in mind for some time as an MI5 agent. He was felt to be a good person to contact Hess. Yet according to Richard Deacon, a historian of the time, Crowley was known to the Germans as an intelligence suspect from his time in the early 1930s in Germany. This was because Crowley had shared a flat with Gerald Hamilton who was a notorious spy. Crowley was spying on Hamilton for MI5 and Hamilton was spying on Crowley for the Germans! However at that time Hamilton had claimed he was spying on Crowley for the British! Which was true? Baffling counterintelligence !
Crowley was allowed to assist in England by preparing the Astrological Chart for Hess. This plan was abandoned when Rudolph Hess flew to Scotland in May 1941. He parachuted to Britain to commence negociations on Germany's behalf. Ian Fleming proposed that Crowley would be a good negociator to look into the extent of the influence of Astrology on various Nazi leaders. The Admiralty would not allow this to happen. However Ian Fleming included Aleister Crowley in his first James Bond novel, 'Casino Royale' of 1953. His villain 'Le Chiffre' was modelled partly on Crowley - Maxwell Knight became the Chief 'M'.

MAXWELL KNIGHT

IAN FLEMING

In 1940 Crowley moved to 57 Petersham Road, Richmond and stayed there during the Summer to avoid the bombing in Central London and improve his asthma.

The back of Petersham Road, Richmond in Surrey, overlooking the Thames.

Though bombing raids were frequent in London at this time, and aggravated Crowley's asthma, he also found them exhilarating. Camell visited him at this time and wrote, "...As dawn broke we drank our stirrup cup, or night cap - the toast 'Damnations to Dictators!' I went home for a few hours sleep. Crowley, his asmatha cured by the blazing bomber, slept like a child".

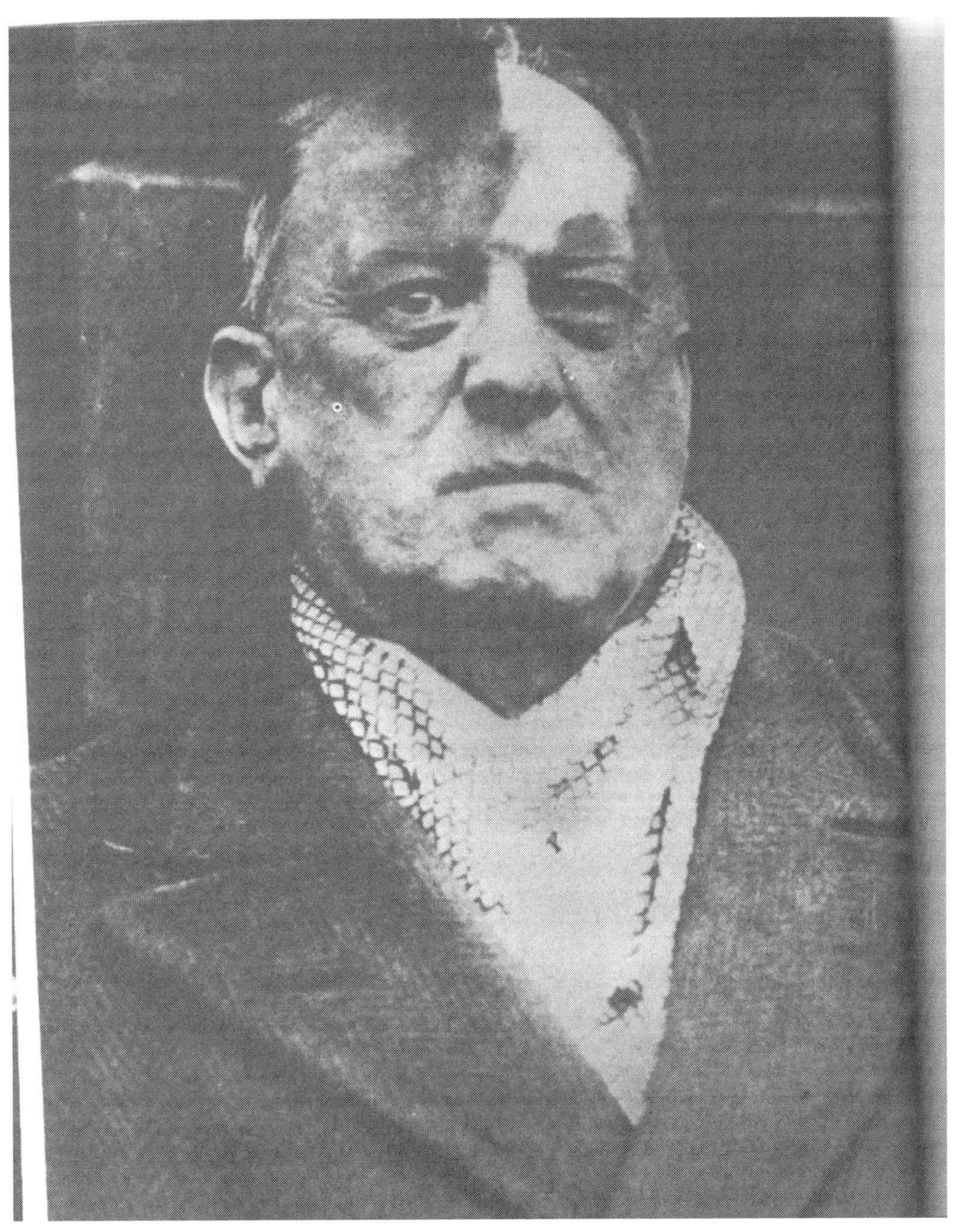

Crowley at Cleopatra's Needle in London

At this time moneymaking schemes occurred to Crowley such as a board game called 'Thelema'. Another was to open a 'Magick Restaurant' with spicey dishes such as those from Mexico, Tunisia and India and other places he had visited. It was well know that Crowley loved curries!

Charles R Cammell visited Crowley again at 57 Petersham Road during the Summer of 1940. There was a bombing raid and the anti-aircraft guns hit a German bomber which fell to earth in flames. Cammell later wrote that Crowley "…. ran downstairs two steps at a time and was shouting Hooray! And waving his arms skyward in a passion of boyish excitement and jubilation. He had no trace of asthma, it was gone whence it came. Crowley was 21 again…"

But sadly Cammell and Crowley fell out the following year. Crowley refused to pay Cammell's wife Iona for a large quantity of tweed cloth which she had hand-woven and he had ordered. Cammell was sad to lose the friendship with Crowley but wrote of him, "I did my best to arrange matters, to persuade him to act honourably or at least reasonably and courteously. It was useless. As was his wont when challenged, he became defiant. In some such way he lost many of his best friends; George Cecil Jones, Eckenstein, Mathers, Allan Bennett, General Fuller, Sir Gerald Kelly, Victor Neuberg. They were each in turn compelled to break with Crowley, even as I was. I saw him only once again - in London, after the War. We did not speak".

Crowley's asthma grew worse as did his heroin use. He was lovers with a woman called Alice Upton during 1940 but their relationship was stormy and eventually fell apart. Crowley decided to leave Richmond and London for the tranquillity of Torquay where he resided at The Gardens, Middle Warberry Road for six months. He wrote to Yorke at this time:
" I wish you had always understood me. I could have worked out the details with you. But there was a time when you distrusted me entirely; a lot of it my own fault. Is it too late to get together heart and soul? 'Trust not a stranger ;fail not an heir'. I feel so lonely, like a frightened child. So much to do and my physical instrument untrusty!" Yet Crowley had more problems with rent and so moved to Barton Brow in April 1941. He showed interest in 2 women at this time Mildred Churt and and Grace M Pennel. Though neither of these relationships were deep or long standing. In June he found he could not perform sexually at all with Alice Upham. So in October 1941, Crowley returned to London and lived alone at a flat at 10 Hanover Square.

Hanover Square Today

CROWLEY'S FINEST ACHIEVEMENT - THE TAROT FOR THE NEW AEON

The Wheel begins to turn

Aleister Crowley first met Lady Frieda Harris in 1937 when she was 60 and married to Sir Percy Harris the Liberal MP. She was introduced to him by Clifford Bax who moved in theatrical circles! She was an artist and had aspirations of spiritual and magical development. As a result she was initiated into the Ordo Templis Orientis (OTO). Crowley asked her to work with him on designing a new Tarot Deck and this was the basis of her magical training. Their friendship and relationship as student and teacher lasted for the next 10 years until Crowley passed away in 1947. It was the most enduring of his accomplishments and today would surely have made him the rich man he craved to be.

Crowley and Lady Frieda Harris with a friend in a stripped dress c.1939

Curiously Crowley estimated originally that it would take Frieda a day each for the 40 minor arcana cards and 2 days each for the 16 Court Cards, It was to take half a week each for the 22 major arcana cards. On the outside 6 months was allowed; which showed that he had no idea of the task and its magnitude, which eventually spanned four years. Frieda wrote to him, "One hundred years for each card would have been the right time", with an artists' flourish, but she made it clear to him in 1938, "If you could only stop believing that I am a rich and vulnerable, middle-aged, middle-class woman, whose vanity, quite possibly, Is there to be used, then we could go on. I cannot get you out of this mess. I want this job done quickly and as well as I can, but if we can't do it, Alright! I will do something else. Could you stop associating me with your financial debris, as I can't help you!"

Frieda was paying Crowley for her instruction and she wrote to him from Morton House, the Mall, Chiswick on 10th May 1939,
"My Dear Aleister, your secretary forgot to send the letter you wrote to me and she has rung me up to read it to me. I am also sorry that I have to write plainly to you because I enjoy your friendship and your instruction very much but it is entirely spoilt by your attempts to use me as your bank and financial adviser. I have frequently told you that I have nothing but a weekly allowance and that Out of it I have given you all that I can spare. If you are expecting the Tarot to be a means of getting money or my position to be useful, then I am sorry I am not the right vehicle for such an enterprise as I intend to remain anonymous When the cards are shown as I dislike any notoriety".

Morton House, The Mall Chiswick

Lady Frieda Harris took herself off to the British Museum every day for some weeks in 1938 to delve into the History of Tarot. At the same time she wrote almost daily to Crowley about the cards, their composition, colour and symbolism. Crowley was working on The Book of Thoth and sent her some of the draft copies of what he had written. She wrote back , "Your book is wonderful but I cannot understand most of it as I do not know its secret language............The Fool is a great dignitary. My hand trembles before him. I wish I could convey it in a more simple line....."

Reading Room, The British Museum

Crowley had some of his work published in 1939. He was pleased with this but became very ill this year and had to be sent to a private nursing home. Frieda Pawned some of her personal possessions to pay for this. She kept this from her husband. As Crowley slowly recovered she found him a flat in Petersham Road, Richmond, Surrey, which was not far from Morton House.

43 - 47 Petersham Road, Richmond Surrey

These were the dark and uncertain days at the beginning of the War when rationing had started to be introduced and the Americans had not decided on which side they stood. Crowley and Frieda tried to block out the World in their struggle to complete the Great Work but in the Autumn she wrote again to Crowley, "I am in distress about money, Percy has reduced my allowance by half. He is hit by the taxes and also requires any available cash to finance his personal message. I do not think I shall be able to hold on to my flat in Richmond very much longer......I have done all the swords except the 3 - And partly 4 - I am sure I shall be done by Christmas....I have finished the 5 of Swords. I don't like it much. No 9 is alright. It is much easier to work in the studio (in Gloucestershire), and I am not restless at all, thank you........"

Crowley wrote to Frieda from 57 Petersham Road, Richmond on 19th December 1939, "Dear Frieda, Do what thou wilt, shall be the whole of the Law.

Benediction arrived this morning from Father Jackson. I am very happy and grateful. I was going to send you a 'Classic of Purity' Liber XXII but I have not yet been able to get the special copy that I had intended for you. I have been terrifically worried. I have not had a word from Germer since his letter of 30th November, and this is very unusual. Normally I hear at least once and sometimes twice a week. This has meant continuous anxiety and frustration. My characteristic idiocy has just been giving another demonstration. I have been wondering for a week why it hurt to carry coal upstairs, and it only dawned upon me last night that it was lumbago, so I then turned on the infra-red and it was alright in half an hour. This is a very strange thing about me, something goes wrong which is perfectly familiar, and I know the remedy quite well, and I am simply unable to put two and two together. I don't know why that is. A queer psychological kink................" In fact Crowley was ill and growing old. His forgetfulness was a sign of Old Age and his limbs and strength were failing him. In 1940 he was 65 and not a fit 65, but an ill 65. Good health at this time would have carried him through to 85 or 90 and we should have had him around til 1960 or 1965 by which time he would have been an aged and respected voice of Knowledge and Sage-like Wisdom. Suffice to say, 1940 was the year of strongest collaboration between Lady Frieda Harris and Crowley on the creation of the Tarot Cards. This is detailed in 'My Dear Aleister' by the current author.

In May 1942 Crowley moved back to the West End of London to a flat in Hamilton House, 140 Piccadilly. He missed central London and loved to be in the thick of things.

Hamilton House, 140 Piccadilly

He and Lady Frieda Harris succeeded in staging two exhibitions of the Tarot Cards as paintings. The first was at the Berkeley Galleries at 20 Davies Street, Mayfair, in July 1942.

20 Davies Street, now a food and wine shop

The second exhibition was at the Royal Society of Painters of Water Colours, In August 1942. A friend of Crowley's, Robert Cecil hoped to persuade T S Eliot who worked as an editor at Faber & Faber to publish the manuscript of the Book of Thoth. Though this did not happen. Crowley was also in touch with the Agape Lodge of the OTO in Los Angeles at this time where later trouble was to brew. It was also this Autumn that Crowley went to New Bond Street to record on wax cylinders his 'Hymn to Pan', as sound recording was in its infancy. He went to Levy's Sound Studios to do this.

There was another artistic field that Crowley dipped into at the invitation of a new young theatre director. Peter Brook contacted Crowley as he was staging a production of Dr Faustus at the Torch Theatre in Oxford, in October 1942. He had read some of Crowley's writings on Magick and wrote to Crowley to ask him about staging various scenes in the play. Crowley attended one or two rehearsals. He was invited to the opening night and announced "All considered , an A1 performance - it held the audience". Crowley and Lady Frieda Harris continued their work on the Tarot Cards during the rest of 1942 and during 1943. During the Winter of 1943 he moved to a new address at 93 Jermyn Street. His Landlady was a Miss Manning who conducted séances and later named a room after Crowley for the use of her mediumistic work. Their relationship went downhill as his rent payments to her declined.

Crowley lived above this food store

Crowley remarked at this time that his sexual energy was in total decline. He felt weak due to the lack of this function. Perhaps it was for this reason that he dealt with the Master of Agape Lodge OTO in Los Angeles, Wilfred Talbot Smith, so harshly. Their relationship through correspondence had previously been amicable for over 10 years. However, Smith had seduced Helen Parsons, the wife of Jack Parsons, another Lodge member. Parsons was a brilliant scientist and helped to develop rocket fuel. Parsons seemed to get over this domestic matter. He began an affair with his wife's sister Sarah Elizabeth. At this time in his life Crowley became worried about the reputation of the OTO! Rumours had lead to an FBI investigation of the Agape Lodge. Crowley's hypocritical attitude was, to say the least, unhelpful and a little astounding. However Smith was sent on a Great Magical Retirement at a place called 'Rancho Royal' in October 1943.

Crowley designated Parsons as the new Master of Agape Lodge. Sadly Smith wrote repentant letters to Crowley! Parsons tendered his resignation of the Agape Lodge to Crowley and accused Crowley of pomposity and blundering leadership; so all ended in the usual manner thanks to Crowley's meddling.

Jack Parsons

Crowley's lack of trust in those he worked or collaborated with, culminated in a letter to the Sun Engraving Company, complaining about Lady Frieda Harris and her organisation of the printing of the cards. There was almost a legal development out of this disagreement but luckily no court case ensued. Frieda was merely trying to get the cards made and put before the public. The whole deck was completed in 1944, the final card being Adjustment which is also called Justice. As the cards were completed Frieda needed Crowley less but he needed her more. He became increasingly more ill and frail over the next 2 years and she arranged for him to be looked after and nursed, and also visited him. The Book of Thoth was published by the Chiswick Press on 21st March 1944 with assistance from Grady Louis McMurtry who was the new potential leader of the Agape Lodge OTO in California. McMurtry had called upon Crowley whilst in England at 93 Jermyn Street, and they both remained in correspondence during the War.

Grady Louis McMurtry

Originally there were 200 signed and numbered copies, leather bound. Crowley wrote of the Tarot, "Each card is in a sense, a living being; and its relations with its neighbours are what one might call diplomatic. It is for the student to build these living stones into his living temple". The Book of Thoth sold for 10 guineas a copy. It was a Triumph of magical work and combined Crowley's knowledge, not just of sex magic, but also of colour, of numerology, of astrology and the Kabbalah, the Tree of Life. That it was completed during WW2 is perhaps its best time to be written. Created by a Magician who was shunned by the World around him he created his World anew through the Tarot and the Book of Thoth, for the New Aeon.

But Crowley's health was still declining in Winter 1943 and Frieda Harris persuaded him to get a Nurse for his care. He was using 4 to 6 grains of heroin a day in 1943 and 1944 and roughly 10 grains during the first half of 1945. This was on prescription along with cocaine and veronal and eythl oxide.

At this time he also had a new female student Anne Macky also named Soror Fiat Yod who had a strong interest in Magick. Crowley wrote to Macky about Magick to spur on her interest. She gave him the idea to write a book entitled, 'Aleister Explains Everything', which eventually became, 'Magick Without Tears' and Germer published these papers posthumously in 1954.

The bombing of London in 1944 drove Crowley to seek a safer home outside of London again. He moved to the Bell Inn in the small village of Aston Clinton, in Buckinghamshire. Certainly nearer to Frieda in Gloucestershire, for meeting up and discussing the launching of the Tarot.

The attractive Bell Inn at Ashton Clinton, Bucks. Still open today

Whilst at the Bell Inn, Crowley had an RAF Squadron for company who had been posted there. He also had a sympathetic landlady, Daphne Harris - no relation to Lady Frieda! Being the joker that Crowley was he asked his Nurse one day to take a hatchet to be sharpened, which terrified the life out of her. Life was fine for a while.

But declining relations with his landlady led Crowley to seek out another and final home. He had at times been in the kitchen taking sugar and other food during a time of rationing. His stay at the Bell Inn, Ashton Clinton was at an end. Friends sought a new and more permanent home for him to settle in.

THE JOURNEY HOMEWARD

Crowley in the Garden at Netherwood

Tao Te Ching by Aleister Crowley: The Way Of Heaven
'The Tao of Heaven is likened to the bending of a bow, whereby the high part is brought down, and the low part raised up. The extreme is diminished, and the middle increased. This is the Way of Heaven, to remove excess, and to supplement insufficiency. Not so is the way of Man, who taketh away from him that hath not to give, to him that hath already excess.
Who can employ his own excess to the wealth of all under heaven? Only he that possesseth the Tao. So the Wise Man acteth without lust of result; achieveth and boasteth not; he willeth not to proclaim his greatness'

Crowley towards the end of his Life started to create a sense of Peace in his world as his health placed more and more demands on him. Thus when there is a balance of yin and yang, the wholeness of a personal universe is created. Feng Shui comes into play - the balance of Wind and Water. Travelling West, North West or South West was always beneficial for Crowley. Now he travelled South to Hastings and to Netherwood. The I Ching or Book of Changes had been consulted. In the past learned mandarins had acquired the knowledge of the I Ching and Feng Shui. These men were much like magicians and enjoyed privileged positions at court, particularly under the Tang Emperor (AD 888). They were consulted when palaces and tombs were built; they studied landscapes and calculated compass directions as well as studying birth dates.

Crowley the Magus and Mandarin was going to his final home, on a hill and close to the sea for Crowley could not stay long away from water. His new landlord and landlady were Vernon and Johnny (female) Symonds a lively , middle aged couple; Vernon was a playwright and actor and the couple wanted to create a unique atmosphere in their boarding house.

Netherwood, Hastings - courtesy of Deslan

Netherwood, was on The Ridge and private, surrounded by trees. Crowley could smoke his strong tobacco here and drink his sugary tea. It was here that John Symonds came to interview him whilst writing Crowley's biography, The Great Beast. But Crowley was a shadow of the man he had once been. Still injecting heroin daily, his liver and kidneys must have been almost depleated. Crowley's room was Number 13 and he spent most of the day in it after breakfast at 9am. Visitors came to see him often; Louis Wilkinson, Robert Cecil, Lady Frieda Harris, and Michael Houghton who at that time owned the Atlantis Bookshop in Museum Street, Bloomsbury, London. It was Louis Wilkinson's son Oliver who found Netherwood for Crowley, and Louis Wilkinson who helped to edit commentarys on the Book of the Law.

Yet Crowley was not finished with his teaching of students. A young man of 20 , Kenneth Grant wrote to Crowley in 1945. Crowley asked Grant to come and live at Netherwood in a cottage in the grounds, and he , Grant, would help to serve his Master Therion. Grant described Crowley as a 'fragile ivory figure of a mandarin.....hands slightly yellow...curiously small'; he had shrunk from his former obesity. Kenneth Grant studied well under Crowley and page by page, but Crowley would not tell him anything about the sex magic doctrine until he had completed the 9th degree OTO. Eventually he came to know this.
Grant obtained drugs for Crowley, or whisky, and managed his everyday affairs. By his own admission he wasn't well suited to this personal assistant post, and returned to London as his father wanted him to take up a career, in June 1945. Before he went Austin Spare did a sketch of him, and Crowley regarded Kenneth Grant as the potential future leader of the OTO.

Kenneth Grant by Austin Spare

During these last two years John Symonds describes to us how bored Crowley was as in his notes. Crowley wrote of "long, lonely boring evenings"...."It's boredom and Anno Domini. A girl or a game of chess would fill the gap. But I've just not enough pep to start research...........lost valuables and careless folly. What an ass I am! Will heroin help me forget?" And his daily intake of heroin rose to as many as eleven grains at this time.

Dion Fortune also came to see Crowley at Netherwood. He had first met her at The Belfry in London , in March 1939. Hugo Astley a character in her novel 'The Winged Bull' was based on Crowley. Dion Fortune was a wise enough woman to see Crowley as the man he was, rather than the press-created figure. She had read his books and felt a respect for him which was reciprocated by Crowley. Dion Fortune died from leukaemia in January 1946. She wrote to Crowley up until the end and both shared a complete dedication to Magick.

Dion Fortune was a magical High Priestess with her own magical path. She admired and respected Crowley and the Law of Thelema, even though it wasn't On her path.

Dion Fortune

Gerald Gardner

Another important and influential visitor to Netherwood in 1947 was Gerald Gardner. Gardner was the founder of the Witchcraft or Wicca movement. Gardner was widely travelled and a former British Customs Officer in Malaya. He was initiated into a coven in 1939 and owned and operated a Museum of Witchcraft and Magic on the Isle of Man. In 1954 he published 'Witchcraft Today' which was taken up with much interest in England and America.. He wrote 'The Book of Shadows' in the 1940s which described witchcraft rites. Gardner paid Crowley £300 for OTO fees and duties at this time and was issued an OTO Charter by Crowley and signed by him. It entitled Gardner to set up an OTO chapter, but this he never did. One thing we must now note however is the Gardner drew heavily on Crowley's writings when he wrote, 'The Book of Shadows'. Doreen Valiente rewrote, 'The Book of Shadows' and cut out much of the Crowleyanity, at Gardners' request. Gardner seems to have been under the impression that Crowley was a member of a coven when he was much younger, Though this seems unlikely and there is no evidence for this in all the Crowley information about him. The time mentioned is 1899 - 1900, a time when Crowley had just joined the Order of the Golden Dawn and was preparing to work his way up in the ranks of Magicians.

Another writer visited Crowley in Netherwood in his final years. Elizabeth Butler was writing, 'The Myth of the Magus' about Crowley and had read several of his books. She was a Professor at Cambridge University and went nervously to meet him on 1st January 1946. Crowley met her in the front hall of Netherwood and seemed very old and decomposing to her. "His face was yellow and his voice was the ugliest thing about him, thin, fretful and scratchy - a pedantic voice and a pretentious manner". Crowley took her to his bed-sitting room for the interview. He was hoping for a positive mention in her book. His personal things were strewn about his bedroom and stacked paintings by a wall, Butler turned her nose up at this. However when her book was published in 1946 he was barely mentioned and dismissed as a failed Satanist. Unfortunately in her interview she was not engaging as a researcher but rather frightened and repulsed by Crowley. Crowley told her that 'Magic is not a way of Life, it is The Way of Life'. She dismissed him as a drug addicted old Crow who was totally over-rated. Yet for all his poverty, and living on the kindness of friends, she was unable to see that he was a brilliant man, an intellectual and someone who had pushed the boundaries of reality and Science to produce Magic, which lead him to become a Magus and a Guru, no matter what he now no longer owned or had. Society had reduced him, to this poverty at the end of his Life, and revealed its scorn and complacency with his original thinking. This high flying and patronising Professor Butler, down from Cambridge saw an ill and drug addicted Magician fallen on the worst of hard times. She was devoid of compassion, and lacking in objectivity. She did not ask the right questions because she didn't know the questions to ask. She was the archetypal writer or journalist the Press had always used against the Great Beast.

But the Great Beast was not as frail as he looked and was able to put Jack Parsons on track regarding his life and work at the Agape Lodge, in Pasadena, California, where he had taken over as leader. Jack wrote to Crowley, in July 1945
"About 3 months ago I met Ron Hubbard. He is a writer and explorer; a gentleman. He has red hair, green eyes and is honest and intelligent and we have become great friends. He moved in with me about 2 months ago, and although Betty and I are still friendly, she has transferred her sexual affection to Ron. I cared for her rather deeply but I have no desire to control her emotions. Although Ron has no formal training in Magick, he has an extraordinary amount of experience and understanding in the field. From some of his experiences I deduced that he is in direct touch with some higher intelligence possibly his Guardian Angel. He describes his Angel as a beautiful winged woman with red hair whom he calls the Empress...He is the most Thelemic person I have ever met and is in complete accord with our own principles. He is also interested in establishing the New Aeon".

Crowley's intuition was second to none on this matter and he warned Parsons against Ron L Hubbard. Parsons began a series of magical workings called the Babalon Workings to obtain for himself a new magical partner. On 23 February 1946 Parsons wrote to Crowley that he now had obtained his new magical partner and she had red hair and green eyes as he had asked for. She was an artist and her name was Marjorie Cameron. Parsons continued to keep Hubbard in the group and wrote to Crowley that he had achieved a new Guardian through a sexual working with Cameron. This being had been channelled through Ron L Hubbard. Crowley was concerned and wrote to Germer, "Apparently Parsons or Hubbard or somebody is producing a Moonchild. I get fairly frantic when I contemplate the idiocy of these goats!"
But it was the earthly plane which broke Jack Parsons from Ron L Hubbard. Parsons, Hubbard and Betty had formed a business called 'Allied Enterprises'. They would jointly buy yachts on the East Coast then sail them to California and sell them for a profit. Parsons put up all of his savings for this but the business

fell apart. In July he filed a suit against Ron L Hubbard and Betty. A settlement was made and from then on Betty and Ron L Hubbard were out of Parsons life. Sadly Parsons died in an accident whilst working alone at a laboratory on 20th June 1952.

Ron L Hubbard

Crowley at Netherwood was completing his list of wishes and dreams. He wrote to Gerald Yorke about having a book of his poems published. "...I have picked out 54 poems, all as different as possible and all written in as many different parts of the Northern Hemisphere as possible". 'Olla' was published by the OTO in December 1946, a limited edition of 500 copies with a frontispiece by Augustus John.

Another visitor to Crowley at Netherwood was the author James Laver who had written a biography of Nostrodamus. He was also the Keeper of Prints and Drawings at the Victoria and Albert Museum. Crowley told Laver Magick was something we do ourselves. "It is more convenient to assume the objective existence of an Angel who gives us new knowledge, than to allege that our invocation has awakened a supernatural power in ourselves".

James Laver

Bit by bit he was rounding off his life and closing some chapters. Some friends had moved abroad, some he had broken off with, many he had treated churlishly, and unforgivingly. What great hopes he had had for his poetry and writing at Eastbourne School! And how he had hoped to scale a mountain and make a name for himself! Did he chose Magick or did it chose him?

Crowley as a younger man in America

He wrote an emotional letter to his son Ataturk before he died. Ataturk was at this time 12 years old. Crowley had been 11 when his own father died.

He asked that he pay attention to his handwriting and write well paying attention to the reader. He told him of the Crowley family lineage that could date back to the 15th century Duke of La Querouaille of France, and asked him to behave as a Duke might possibly behave. Ataturk he asked to learn Latin and Greek and also Chess. He also asked him to learn parts of the Old Testament and Shakespeare which would equip him with the best of English writing. Ataturk was named Aleister Ataturk MacAlpine and did not take Crowley's name.

Louis Wilkinson as the loyal friend he was looked after Aleister Crowley until he passed away and into Spirit. He died on 1st December 1947 at Netherwood, from Myocardial Degeneration and severe Bronchitis. His suffering from his asthma, illness and drug addiction ceased. He had done everything that he could do. Patricia MacAlpine was there when he passed away and said his death came quietly. A gust of wind and a peal of thunder were heard outside. It was the Gods greeting him!" Patricia MacAlpine said. She had brought Aleister Ataturk and her other children to see him before he passed.

REQUIEM

Aleister Crowley was cremated at Brighton Crematorium on 5th December 1947, on a cold grey afternoon so typical of December skies in Britain. Louis Wilkinson read out the 'Hymn to Pan' and from 'The Book of the Law' and the 'Gnostic Mass'. Those attending included Lady Frieda Harris and Gilbert Bayley, also Sister Ilyarum and Brothers Volo Intelligere and Aossic, Gerald Yorke and Louis Wilkinson. The poet Kenneth Hopkins came, who had not know Crowley in Life.

Brighton & Hove Crematorium

In sorting out the estate Louis Wilkinson wrote to Germer that Crowley had left £460, £30 of which was in old bank notes which would have to be changed for current ones. Wilkinson was hoping to pay the Symond's at Netherwood for Crowley's room and board and also a printers. However the Official Receivers had pounced like hawks and would not allow any of his goods, papers & books or paintings and belongings which had been stored at Whiteleys, to be moved. Whiteleys was a Department Store in Bayswater, London . In the same breath, when Lady Frieda Harris and Louis Wilkinson went to Whiteleys they found that the bill for storage had not been paid and so had to pay them £44 or they would have sold Crowleys' worldly goods. Germer was also told that the cash was in a bank account at Lloyds in Hastings. The Official Receiver had put a block on withdrawals until the debts of the Bankruptcy and later debts had been paid. Lady Frieda Harris and Louis Wilkinson were the executors and signatories of this account. Germer said he would offer a lump sum of £300 to the Official Receiver for the bankruptcy so that Crowley's belongings could be released and sent over to him in America.

The tying up of loose ends took over 2 years. On 17th June 1948 Louis Wilkinson wrote to Lloyds Bank that the Official Receiver had relinquished claims to Crowley's money and that the £460 should be transferred to a deposit account. On 3rd December 1948 Louis Wilkinson wrote again to Germer, a year after Crowley's death. He informed him that he had paid Deidre Mac Alpine £37 and also discussed Aleister Ataturk's education with her. Finally on 21st January 1950 Wilkinson wrote to Germer to say that the money in the account had been rounded off. He had paid Deidre MacAlpine £10 and the War Credit Bond had amassed £50. Even now the Inland Revenue were trying to get their hands on This last £50.

Base Camp Kanchengunga

The Excellence of Mystery - from the Tao Te Ching

"Who Knoweth the Tao keepeth Silence' ,he who babbleth knoweth it not
Who knoweth it closeth his mouth and controlled the Gates of his Breath.
He will make his sharpness blunt; he will loosen his complexes; he will tone down his brightness to the general obscurity. This is called the Secret of Harmony.
He cannot be insulted either by familiarity or aversion; he is immune to ideas of gain or loss, of honour or disgrace; he is the true man, unequalled under Heaven".

The above impression is by Psychic Artist Victoria Neal. Victoria was working with me at a Psychic Fayre in Cambridge on 24th September 2007. It was a slow Sunday morning and I noticed Victoria, who was on a stand opposite to me, working away furiously on a new drawing. She brought it over to me when she had finished and said, "This is for you Marlene. I saw this man standing behind you and had to capture him for you". To me it was, undoubtedly Crowley.
He was wanting to be noticed and was wanting to be remembered. He seems to have a Mona Lisa smile on his face and a twinkle in his eye. He is both dark and light, calm and energised. He has reached a point of balance in his spiritual journey. Love is the Law, Love under will.

BIBLIOGRAPHY

Tao Te Ching - Lao Tzu; Aleister Crowley, Wilder Publications 2008
The Book of Thoth - Aleister Crowley; Samuel Weiser 1982 ed.
The Book of the Law - Aleister Crowley; Red Wheel/Weiser 2004
The Book of Lies - Aleister Crowley; Red Wheel/Weiser 1981
The Diary of a Drug Fiend - Aleister Crowley; Red Wheel/
Do What Thou Wilt - A Life of Aleister Crowley; Lawrence Sutin 2000
The Great Beast - John Symonds; MacDonald & Co 1971
The Rough Guide to Sicily - Robert Andrews & Jules Brown, Rough Guides 2005
The Tao Te Ching - John R Mabry; Element 1995
Chinese Divination - Sasha Fenton ; Zambezi 2001
Chinese Elemental Astrology - E Crawford & T Kennedy; Piatkus 1992
I Ching or Book of Changes - Richard Wilhelm (trans), Arkana 1989
The Magical Dilemma of Victor Neuberg - Jean Overton Fuller; Mandrake 2005
The Middle Pillar - Israel Regardie
The Aleister Crowley Scrapbook - Sandy Robertson; Foulsham & Co 1988
The Tarot - Richard Cavendish; Chancellor Press 1987
The Black Arts - Richard Cavendish; Picador 1977
The Cefalu Diaries 1920-23 - Jane Wolfe - College of Thelema/Lulu.com 2010
My Dear Aleister - Creating the Crowley Harris Tarot; Marlene Packwood Lulu.com 2009
The Cosmic Arcana - Marlene Packwood; Lulu.com 2010
The Feng Shui Kit - Man-Ho Kwok; Piatkus 1998
The Feng Shui Workbook - Wu Xing; Piatkus 1998
I Ching - Will Adcock; New Life Library/ Anner Pub. 2001
Chinese Astrology - Man-Ho Kwok - Tuttle Pub. 1997
The Fundamentals of Feng Shui - Lillian Too; Element 1999
The Personal Feng Shui Manual - Master Lam Kam Chuen; Gaia Books 1998
The Complete Illustrated Guide to Feng Shui - Lillian Too; Element 1996
Feng Shui from Scratch - Jonathan Dee ; D & S Books 2002
The Sacred East - Ed. C Scott Littleton - Duncan Baird Pub. 1996
Plan Your Home With Feng Shui - Ian Bruce - Quantum 1998
The Feng Shui Handbook - Derek Walters - Aquarian Press 1991

With Special Thanks to my son Stephen for his help with layout And for the cover. Caital Design. Thanks go also to Victoria Neal, Psychic Artist of Green Rose.org. Thanks to Deslan for the use of the Netherwood photo.

Printed in Great Britain
by Amazon

74645332R00079